Hydrojustice

Theory Redux series
Series editor: Laurent de Sutter

Published Titles
Mark Alizart, *Cryptocommunism*
Armen Avanessian, *Future Metaphysics*
Franco Berardi, *The Second Coming*
Alfie Bown, *The Playstation Dreamworld*
Alfie Bown, *Post-Comedy*
Laurent de Sutter, *Narcocapitalism*
Diedrich Diederichsen, *Aesthetics of Pop Music*
Mladen Dolar, *Rumors*
Roberto Esposito, *Persons and Things*
Boris Groys, *Becoming an Artwork*
Graham Harman, *Immaterialism*
Helen Hester, *Xenofeminism*
Srećko Horvat, *The Radicality of Love*
Lorenzo Marsili, *Planetary Politics*
Fabian Muniesa, *Paranoid Finance*
Dominic Pettman, *Infinite Distraction*
Eloy Fernández Porta, *Nomography*
Andreas Philippopoulos-Mihalopoulos, *Hydrojustice*
Mikkel Bolt Rasmussen, *Late Capitalist Fascism*
Gerald Raunig, *Making Multiplicity*
Helen Rollins, *Psychocinema*
Avital Ronell, *America*
Nick Srnicek, *Platform Capitalism*
Grafton Tanner, *Foreverism*
Oxana Timofeeva, *Solar Politics*
Alenka Zupančič, *Disavowal*

Hydrojustice

Andreas Philippopoulos-Mihalopoulos

polity

Copyright © Andreas Philippopoulos-Mihalopoulos 2025

The right of Andreas Philippopoulos-Mihalopoulos to be identified as Author of this Work has been asserted in accordance with the UK Copyright, Designs and Patents Act 1988.

First published in 2025 by Polity Press

Polity Press
65 Bridge Street
Cambridge CB2 1UR, UK

Polity Press
111 River Street
Hoboken, NJ 07030, USA

All rights reserved. Except for the quotation of short passages for the purpose of criticism and review, no part of this publication may be reproduced, stored in a retrieval system or transmitted, in any form or by any means, electronic, mechanical, photocopying, recording or otherwise, without the prior permission of the publisher.

ISBN-13: 978-1-5095-6163-6
ISBN-13: 978-1-5095-6164-3(pb)

A catalogue record for this book is available from the British Library.

Library of Congress Control Number: 2024948791

Typeset in 12.5 on 15pt Adobe Garamond
by Cheshire Typesetting Ltd, Cuddington, Cheshire
Printed and bound in Great Britain by CPI Group (UK) Ltd, Croydon

The publisher has used its best endeavours to ensure that the URLs for external websites referred to in this book are correct and active at the time of going to press. However, the publisher has no responsibility for the websites and can make no guarantee that a site will remain live or that the content is or will remain appropriate.

Every effort has been made to trace all copyright holders, but if any have been overlooked the publisher will be pleased to include any necessary credits in any subsequent reprint or edition.

For further information on Polity, visit our website:
politybooks.com

Contents

Acknowledgements   vii

1   Hydra   1
    Wavewriting I: A Hydrojustice Manifesto   32
2   Be Water   35
    Wavewriting II: Mediation   61
3   Water in Water   63
    Wavewriting III: 'Go to the Water' Ritual   87
4   Water Becomes Difference   90
    Wavewriting IV: Repeat   121
5   Wavewriting   123
    Wavewriting V:
    A Contract unto Hydrojustice   136

Notes   140

Acknowledgements

I am indebted to Elias Avramidis, Laurent de Sutter, Ifor Duncan, Thom Giddens, Peter Goodrich, Jan Hogan, Nathan Julius, Jason Katz, Ewa Macura-Nnamdi, Astrida Neimanis, Yoriko Otomo, Andrea Pavoni, and Yusuf Patel for all your wonderful care, comments, and encouragement; deep thanks to Cedric Gilson and Ewa Tomiczek for their valuable help in ideas and cases. With thanks for hospitality to Bar al Canton and Compagnia della Vela (Giuglia and Francesca especially) in Venice, where most of this book was written.

I

Hydra

1

There can be no justice, unless it is hydrojustice.

Justice can no longer be seen as a solely human affair. Its elemental and planetary dimensions must be brought through. Our planet is much less 'Earth' and much more 'Hydrogeos' (from the noun υδρόγειος, which means 'hydroglobe' in modern Greek). Yes, there are earth, air, and fire on our planet. Yes, there are bodies, human and nonhuman, animate and inanimate. Yes, there is a past and a future hidden in the planet's core and spread on its crust. But within it all there is water: airy or brilliant white, cascading or stagnant, threateningly murky or vaginally wet, exhaled or drowning, but always there – aqueous. The element that makes up this planet, its other elements and its bodies, is water.[1]

Hydrojustice is the paradox of individual bodies of water flowing along other individual bodies of water, all of which are part of various collective bodies of water, and ultimately of one larger body of water. The mere fact that this confluence and difference *happens* is hydrojustice. So hydrojustice is not a solution to issues of injustice. Hydrojustice is already here, around and inside us. It is not something to aspire to, a state of justice to come, but a condition to cherish. It is the way things are and the way they carry on. Hydrojustice is not in abeyance, just as our planet is not in crisis. For we can no longer talk about crisis: this is a new and continually changing anthropocenic reality on an already radically altered planet in rapid ecological degradation. Yet, even in this new reality, hydrojustice emerges. Hydrojustice is here. It is not a call to action but to adaptation.

Hydrojustice is how the agency of water takes over.[2] It is the ontological condition of being everywhere and elsewhere at the same time, the distribution across time and space of distance and confluence. Hydrojustice is wet justice and slippery positions, gliding membranes and surface tension that collapse into smoothness. Hydrojustice is the moving and corroded divide between water and flesh, between geology and living beings, and between the decomposition and the recomposition of bodies.

Hydrojustice is a membrane and a passage. It is a dam and a flow. It is skin and its pores.

Hydrojustice is also a method. It shows us when to flow along and when to float away; how to tell when to keep one's distance and when to come together; and how to be at home in both. It is not just a *Mitsein* ('being with') or a way of thinking about identity politics. It is being at ease with both identity and difference. Hydrojustice's main methodological contribution is the palindrome: ebbing and flowing, transgressing and keeping away, becoming permeable and switching to impermeable when ethics around us demands it. It is also a way of thinking, researching, writing, performing: hydrojustice is a diagonal that links bodies of water (material and immaterial, humans and nonhumans, knowledges and practices) that always reside on a horizontal surface of ontological equality. And it advocates light paddling rather than deep breathless immersion, a hesitant positioning, a constant checking: to bring things together diagonally, one needs to embrace the surface.

Hydrojustice means: follow the waters in their confluence and difference, even if this entails an entirely altered humanity.

However abiding, hydrojustice gets regularly buried under the debris of anthropocentrism, colonialism, extractivism and capitalist exploitation, plastic islands and poisoned lakes. We cannot allow ourselves to be complacent. Our work is one of unearthing, in the double sense of revealing what has been hidden and allowing earth to cede priority to the aquatic.

2

I used to dream of those houses whose windows opened to the sea, where the water would be a welcome guest in one's living room. Although I was born and raised near the Aegean Sea, my family home never had an unmediated view of the water. It was always there, but teasingly veiled: our home was on the second row of buildings in the centre of Thessaloniki, Greece's second-largest city, the sea promenade being prohibitively expensive for us. Mine was a privileged childhood in many respects, but also a tantalisingly incomplete one. I spent a large part of my early adolescent afternoons gazing wistfully at the water shimmering through a distant window of the building across the back alley of our apartment. My access to water was always framed by other people's windows or by a rapid succession of breaths of sea air whenever I visited the houses of better located friends and family.

But on those rare visits when the yearning was satisfied and I briefly had uninterrupted access to the open expanse, I found myself becoming restless, embarrassed, even afraid. I did not know what to make of it. It was too vast, too open, too available. I was used to the stealthy beauty of modernist framing: an aquatic rectangle emerging out of grey urban concrete, or a blinding line of reflected sun on the surface of the sea as we drove past the promenade. These waters, mediated, contained, framed, I could deal with. The vastness, no.

Largely North American, Australian, and generally anglophone, the recent blue turn in humanities and social sciences speaks of the ocean, of crossings, of plastic islands that roam over the planet. It deals with an expansive view of water, flirting with purity and unknowability, both urgent and open, disquieting and hopeful. I find that my way of thinking about water is different: in my water there is always mediation, whether human or geographical. I see water always through windows. I imagine water as the bay of Thermaikos licking the Thessalonian promenade I so coveted with its polluted, rubbish-strewn wavelets, itself part of a sea, not an ocean. My water stews in a claustrophobic toxicity, the inevitability of death by chemicals, the always more bloated pesticidal flow; and yet it still feels like home.[3] My water is a bay, quivering in Mediterranean heat. There is very little rain, hardly any snow, and certainly no ice. My water is not an ocean. It is the Mediterranean enclosure, not a vastness across new worlds. It is an archipelago, not a continental shelf. More constancy, less lunar flow. And less leeway.

This affects my hydroproject in ways I cannot change, and perhaps do not wish to: it makes everything more contained, more proximate, more intimate. It works with glimpses and traces rather than the open invitation to battle against ocean waves. It demands a frame at all times, windows through which the vastness can be hinted at but never fully faced, awnings that connect but also separate. My hydroproject offers an ethical scheme of shared flow where all waters become proximate and lend themselves to a tangible affinity; but at the same time it parses the planet into aquatic neighbourhoods where bodies converge amid their desire for and fear of water.

As Mercè Rodoreda writes in her magisterially drenched novel *Death in Spring*, '[t]hat's why they're afraid. They are consumed by the fear of desire.'[4] This is my water: a circularity of fear and desire, a need to stay behind the window and keep on wishing to slide outside.

Water scares me. I need to allow it to puddle. Only then can I write with it.

3

Somewhere among all this there is injustice. Stacks of it. Injustice flashes so vividly, so passionately, everywhere one looks. It makes up the crushing majority of news, scientific analyses, or even theoretical writing on water. This is not surprising: water has been ignored, devalued, polluted, exploited, dumped, extracted, violated, depleted, weaponised. The list is endless and follows the usual logic of nature's exponential colonising by humans.

But please indulge me: my focus here is justice and its instances of emergence. The text is deliberately upbeat, optimistic (albeit in a 'planet doomed beyond recognition' way) – yet also quotidian and rooted in the present. Justice here is an effortless emergence, unlike most of the traditional conceptualisations of justice – such as liberal theories that parse justice out into chunks of procedure, locality, individual rights, and social expectations, or even critical theory that releases justice into the future, into the mythical, or into the space of negative theology, a divine space where justice appears blinding and therefore inaccessible. Here I want to do justice to the everyday, to the folds of the actual that hold justice not as a secret but as a constitutive element of their folding. Justice is already everywhere.

This does not mean that I ignore injustice. Quite the opposite: injustice is always folded within justice, entangled and co-implicated. It is the trigger for my engagement with hydrojustice.

It underscores everything I write. But here I choose to dwell on the just outcome (if and when it comes), the luminous moment of hydrojustice that crowns (some) fights against injustice. Focusing on injustice instead would harbour important risks: first, it would lose sight of the ubiquity of justice; second, it would end up exalting basic attempts at what we can call juridical justice, namely justice connected to rights. Rights of rivers and other water bodies come to mind, as well as questions of distributive justice and reparation, or access to water. While these are important political and legal conquests that often empower marginalised communities,[5] they end up celebrating tiny drops of procedural common sense as justice.

But here I sketch hydrojustice as a sweeping ontological and material condition that only marginally benefits from such juridical nomenclature. Hydrojustice is impervious to the conceit of categorising bodies (granted, for protecting) into bodies of water and bodies of – what? air? land? human? nonhuman? Going beyond these distinctions is pivotal. To quote Massimiliano Tomba on the 2000 Colombian water war, '[t]he extension of rights and legal personhood to animals and nature, often hailed as a sign of legal progress, is an expression of a hypertrophic process of subsumption of the whole realm of life into the legal realm of the state'.[6] Indeed, such developments distract from the all-encompassing hydro-necessities currently present, for which nothing less than a radical recalibration of humanity will do.

Finally, I choose to focus on justice rather than injustice because I do not want to focus on the symptomatology (fear, anger, hate) of our diseases (individualism and territorialism), which, however, underscore everything I discuss in this book. In an inversion of the Deleuzian 'clinical' and 'critical', my clinical is the positive and my critical is an attempt to unearth it. Hydrojustice is a positive state of confluence, a little like floating on the water: just like that, no need to move, swim, try. How do we enable this effortless state to be the planet's constant becoming?

4

Thinking of justice with water is a short leap. In my work on spatial justice, I have argued that justice must be fully spatialised and embodied in order to be relevant.[7] But we know that water is already everywhere: 'all terrestrial bodies are penetrated and enclosed by water owing to its intrinsic partial forces, vaporous state, and ubiquity in the upper part of the planet'.[8] The multiple forms of water 'have *made* cities', as Alex Wafer and Andrea Pavoni remind us, 'almost through their negation, containment and domestication (at least in Western planning logic), but also in their spectral and haunting qualities: the threat of bursting forth'.[9] If, then, this circularity of desire for, and fear of, water is everywhere and in everything, spatialisation and embodiment can only mean an inalienable connection with the element. But the elemental fleshes out the ontology of movement, and with it that of hydrojustice.

Let me take a step back: spatial justice, for me, is the question that arises when two or more bodies desire to move into the same space at the same time. Add water, and everything becomes less adversarial, more inclining towards one another, more lateral. This makes desire more diffused, less targeted in its direction, less claiming in terms of force. But it does not make it irrelevant. Desire still binds all bodies in their flowing together. It just becomes ubiquitous, conative rather than capricious, and more gossamer. This also means that conflict remains ubiquitous. But, in contrast with the question of spatial justice that stresses the antagonistic and focuses on emergences of spatial injustice, hydrojustice brings forth the ontological state of bodies flowing together. By virtue of this state, bodies are more adept at sharing the flow than at pushing other bodies out of the way.

This book is about finding justice with water, using water as a tool for thinking about justice, but also materially implicating water in all the questions of justice. Water is not a metaphor – or at least not a purely linguistic metaphor. Water, as I write below, is a fully *material* metaphor, one embraced here in its multiple dimensions, as element and language.

I would like to structure the hydrojustice question around two concepts: on the one hand a *continuum* with other bodies, and on the other the *ruptures* of this continuum and the emergence of individual bodies. These two are not a binary but a fold, a circularity and a constant sliding between. And the context is as important as the bodies, since our planet, Hydrogeos, is hovering in a temporality of already irreversible disaster.

5

In ancient Greek mythology, Hydra is a monster raised by the goddess Hera with the sole purpose of slaying Heracles. She nestles in the swamps of Lernaea, one of the entrances to the underworld, patiently waiting for just that divinely prescribed encounter. And Heracles is irresistibly summoned: Hydra is his second labour.

While Hydra is eventually defeated, the operation is neither clean-cut nor particularly heroic – at least by comparison with some of Heracles' other labours. Myths work best when heroes prove their heroism by outwitting their adversary. Here the heroic deed is somewhat diluted: realising the enormity of the task, Heracles job-shares with his nephew Iolaus, an otherwise minor mythical character. Assistance notwithstanding, it quickly becomes obvious that this encounter is far from the usual intelligence versus brute force. Rather it is a pluralising, proliferating, promiscuous affair of multiplication and regeneration. Hydra has multiple heads (anything from nine to fifty) and, every time a head is cut, multiple others grow in its place. Not only that, but Hydra's body commands and expands into the surrounding marine life: she sends a giant crab to attack the heroes and distract them.

Heracles and his nephew were chopping for days, simply feeding the proliferation of Hydra's reach. At some point, of course, the mythical narrative must end in triumph, and the most fitting end depicts Heracles defeating Hydra by dipping the sword in her venomous arteries before chopping the other heads. Fitting because immanent and circular: only by delving deeper into the 'Hydraean' element can one defeat Hydra.

So Hydra is not one thing. Hydra is ouroboros-like circularity and aqueous immanence. She is watery multiplicity, aquatic proliferation, liquid excess.[10] Hydra is destiny encountered and destiny reversed. Hydra is monomania and polymorphy. Hydra is toxic and regenerative. Hydra is feminist killjoy and heroine.

Thus, hydrojustice. Not just aquatic justice but justice everywhere and in everything: every head is a new moment of justice sprouting across time and space; mycelial justice, 'ceaselessly wandering outside and beyond its limits ... a body without a body plan',[11] proliferating and spreading, elemental yet multiple, pulsing with water from within and reinstating itself again and again.[12]

But also justice as non-heroic, non-masculine, non-binary, even anti-human; justice as a paradox of self-generation and self-annihilation. No longer obstructed by the objective blindfold of polite society, justice is now screaming 'I am here' from the infinity of Hydra's eyes.

6

A good few centuries after the myth of Hydra, another myth stirs the waters of the Mediterranean. The Most Serene Republic of Venice celebrates its Marriage to the Sea (Sposalizio del Mare). The doge (until 1797, and now the mayor, in full tourist-approved attire and in some sort of caricature of the original suprematist gesture) slides across the lagoon in his gilded mega-ship, the *Bucintoro*, one Sunday every May. He casts a gold ring into the green waters while uttering: 'We espouse thee, O sea, as a sign of true and perpetual dominion.'

This most amphibious city, one of the classic colonial maritime empires of the past, has always understood itself as an aquatic hybrid. The story of its origins is one of despair, the original settlers flying into the shallow waters of the lagoon to escape Germanic attacks from the north. In time, they realise that their mud-rooted homes on stilts protect them from maritime threats too, since the waters are shallow enough to be treacherous to anyone who doesn't know them well. At the core of Venice's open world dominion there folds a closure of intimate local aquatic knowledge.

This paradox between the inside and the outside is decisive for my understanding of hydrojustice. But I would like to put it aside for just a moment and think instead about the significance of this marriage to the sea – by no means limited to Venice but found in abundance across history.[13] Here, just as with Hydra, water is placed in the service of a myth. Just like Hydra, this water is willed into existence for a sole purpose: to subjugate the Venetian colonies. Just like Hydra, the lagoon guards the gateway to a different, intimate world. And, just as with Hydra, no one asks the water what it wants. Hydra's triumph is absolute: only Hydra can kill herself. Humans duly mediate, of course, and the hydro-polymorphy of our planet is systematically poisoned. But in the 'doge marries the sea' scenario the horror is perpetuated, year after year, be it in earnest or in oblivious parody.

The sea is anthropomorphised as a dutiful wife, herself under perpetual dominion, and also an instrument of Venice's perpetual colonial dominion over the world. Would the sea truly want to get married to that doge guy, onboard his grotesquely large ship and wearing that limp phallic headpiece? It doesn't matter. The sea obediently swallows the ring, year in year out, like a bad joke about an oath renewal, while at the same time getting raped by cruise ships, dams, industrial effluents, excavations, venal local governments, and tourist hordes ruthlessly marching on.

Perpetual dominion over the elements, this most Christian narrative of the role of man can also take relatively benign forms, such as the papal attempt to draw 'lines of amity' to demarcate between sovereign territories and secure safety of transmission; or, closer to Venice, the wooden *bricole* that demarcate safe and deep enough routes for boats in the lagoon. But these need to be seen as temporary shifting ruptures in a sea of aquatic continuum. This is hydrojustice's *prima philosophia*, as legal theorist Peter Goodrich puts it: 'there can be no "purpresture", seizure or enclosure of the sea, not so much because it is boundless but because it is everywhere, because it touches all'.[14] Rather than the great dialectics of Enlightenment that closes off, marks, and alienates, hydrojustice weaves a multipronged space of renewal that involves human and nonhuman aquatic bodies. No one gets married here, and no one gets killed by a hero. Perpetual negotiation among bodies is the way hydrojustice materialises its own abiding myth.

This also reveals another indispensable aspect of hydrojustice: it is not just an idea but a practice of continuous negotiation. Think of the way one needs to reposition oneself all the time when in seawater, even when simply standing in the shallows. There is no other way of being in water than constant negotiation. This is never an uncomplicated, predictable movement. Bodies connect through complex affects that determine their positions and movements. Think of how the doge's flaccid bravado spearheads the fear of a whole empire that the sea will swallow them up, as it regularly did and as it does even now, with Venice's precious palazzi and mosaics: a fear that perhaps the way they have been approaching their aquatic existence is not right.

7

Venice features in this book, especially in the way Italo Calvino's Marco Polo admits to Kublai Khan that, whichever city he speaks of, he always and only speaks of Venice.[15] Currently Venice captures the global imagination of wealthy individuals and organisations as well as that of artists and scientists, standing as it does for a symbol of waters rising everywhere. Although predictable, the bias is disappointing, considering the amount of money poured into Venice as opposed to any other sinking island in the Pacific. Still, its function as symbol at the forefront of the climate struggle has its value.

I chose Venice as my other home a few years ago, but in fact I know I had no choice in the matter. When, seventeen years old, I arrived for the first time in Venice, my mind was filled with prefabricated notions about a certain banality of the city itself, with its bridges, canals, romantic hideaways, and global appeal. I was ready to reject it as mere tourist trap.

It took only a few seconds to fall irreversibly in love, only a few steps out of the train station and towards the expanse of water right there. But it wasn't the obvious beauty that delivered the *coup de foudre*. Rather it was the impossibility to cross over to the other side, a liquid moment of Derridean aporia. Venice showed me my limitations: I was part of a society that could not face its amphibian nature. I myself, in awe of water (disclaimer: never a great swimmer), was precisely that society. And Venice was challenging me with every lapping water movement.

The embrace of the negative, the aporia, the rupture, the distance, the departure, the withdrawal is an important feature of hydrojustice. Not everything is flow and confluence. Disagreement and strife emerge at all points. Being bodies of water entails confluence and admixture, but also taking one's distance, withdrawing from one another, and even coming to conflict.

Hydrojustice emerges when bodies position and reposition themselves along one another, so that ruptures remain in the service of the continuum and the continuum remains in the service of ruptures.

8

What I did not know when I first visited Venice, and I still need to remind myself of to this day, is that the canals remain surprisingly shallow. Even when the green, algae-coloured water seems to be concealing fathoms, the canals, given the right water conditions, are barely 150 cm deep, except of course for the grand canal and a few other larger canals. This means that in theory one could walk across, and indeed people could do just that back in time, when bridges were not that common.

Everything plays out on the surface. With this I do not mean that aquatic depths are irrelevant or that I disagree with hydro-theoretical criticisms against focus on the surface and consequent indifference towards the depths. As environmental humanities researcher Stacy Alaimo, for example, correctly writes, 'the emphasis on the transportation surface neglects vertical zones in favor of horizontal trajectories, making the deep seas the void of the void.'[16]

This is true insofar as we focus on transportation, connectivities, trade routes, and colonial lines.

But surface is not superficiality. Surface is where the depths rise and mingle, as the theorist Karen Barad tells us. It is the space of intra-action among bodies of water (material and immaterial bodies, humans and nonhumans, disciplines and practices).[17] Surface is where the corpses of drowned immigrants float, as cultural theorist Federica Mazzara emphasises.[18] Surface is all there is. I think of a surface whose depth is pulled up and made horizontal. Surface is dwelling: even in depths, a body opens a surface on which to move, pause, dissolve.

Surface is where horizontality spreads. Surface is light paddling, bringing forth the horizontality of intra-action. Surface is remembering horizontality even when one is carried by the vertigo of verticality. We need to stay horizontal to displace the verticality of anthropocenic progress. We need to give up on the angst of control. In *Wild Blue Media*, Melody Jue writes: 'like divers who want to "stand up" when they feel out of control underwater, conceptual displacement is about recognizing what terrestrial habits we carry with us through the act of imagining familiar concepts underwater'.[19]

I think, along with legal theorist Margaret

Davies, of a 'networked, ecological, and connective' horizontality;[20] a horizontality without horizon, expectation, or waiting. I think of a flatness devoid of the vertical desire of climbing and reaching up higher, better.

In this book I am dwelling on the surface of things, that is, on the ever-expanding horizontal depth of the surface.

Hydrojustice renders everything a surface of emergence.

9

'How to think with a body of water that is both rising and evaporating, that is finding [it] hard to breathe, as intoxicated, acidifying, overfished, drained of its resources, and turned into a solid border whose crossing is lethal?'[21] Art curator Barbara Casavecchia sets out the paradox: how can one think with something that limits us, poisons us, kills us? How can one think with something that is regularly instrumentalised as a barrier, a dam, venom, a carrier of colonisers, a weaponised wave, a sovereign boundary, a plastic island, the grand depository of our horrors? Indeed, more than about thinking with, the larger question might be: how can one align one's body along this terrifying carrier of justice?

In order to think with water towards an understanding of hydrojustice, I have been inspired by the blue turn literature in humanities and social sciences,[22] specifically on how bodies are both individual agents and parts of collectives – for example Karen Barad's agential separability, Stacy Alaimo's transcorporeality,[23] or Astrida Neimannis's gestationality,[24] among other theories. Hydrojustice draws on Renisa Mawani's 'oceans as method', in that it focuses on unearthing marginalised histories, alternative timescales, and different registers.[25] It is also close to Karin Amimoto Ingersoll's seascape epistemology, a method of thinking with, moving through, and doing with water.[26] Hydrojustice approaches water ontologically, as in Philip Steinberg and Kimberley Peters' more-than-wet ontology,[27] which works through the multiple forms of water as ontological structures in which knowledge is situated.

Hydrojustice, however, differs from these theories in important ways. Hydrojustice is the ontological condition of one's being on the planet: by virtue of being here and sharing in the water continuum, one is by definition justly positioned. Unlike some sort of natural law, hydrojustice is not something that needs to be reinstated at all times. It is an ontological position in which all bodies partake, beyond their volition; it not a horizon to reach, an ideality to strive for. There is no return to hydrojustice, strictly speaking. Rather, it is a question of continuous adjustment and adaptation to conditions: every time, in every new condition, the whole planet changes and hydrojustice grows yet another head. Just as water fills in any gaps, or vapour takes up all space, or ice coagulates in perfect containment of its form, in the same way hydrojustice always adjusts to surrounding conditions and fills whatever surface emerges.

Yet the irreversibility of environmental degradation, the intensification of challenging conditions, and the new demands on what the future human can be pose a grand challenge to the vertical pride of human structures: building, mining, fracking, flying, social hierarchies of every form, geographical imbalances, temperature and water rises, in short: human 'progress' from being upstanding to commanding the whole planet. A new horizontality, both terrifying and relieving, is augured. Adapting to this horizontality, which will eventually and rather inevitably swallow any remaining human suprematist verticalities, is the challenge of hydrojustice. In the process, hydrojustice liberates the diagonal that animates horizontality. Politically, it attempts to unearth Hydra in all its manifestations. In other words it wants to contribute to the conceptual displacement of a way of thinking that has brought about colonialism, capitalism, rampant consumerism, patriarchy, and human supremacy.

10

Ultimately there is only one way to think with water: *becoming* that body of water. Becoming does not mean change. It simply means allowing one's own body of water to emerge through continuum and ruptures with other bodies; following the ethical thrust of hydrojustice as a shared ethics of flow; allowing the emergence and finding one's home in the emergency.

To do this, I have invited water to become the writer of this book. I employ *wavewriting* as my writing method: writing that laps and ebbs without synthesis, letting the meaning be adumbrated rather than declared, the nuances to flood the ideas, the new emergences to be absorbed by the horizontality of the surface and the circularity of the return. More about this method in the final chapter; here it is necessary to warn readers that the definition of hydrojustice keeps morphing across this book – a multiplicity of positions that wash over the reader. Hydrojustice invites the reader to swim tentatively among the wavelets of the book, to take in the whole while allowing the parts to take her or him elsewhere, to drop any resistance to metaphors and allow their materiality to play with their skin, to dive in and out of the text.

II

Ethically, hydrojustice is the necessity to maintain the ontological condition of aqueous horizontality even at the cost of abandoning human verticality, namely humanity the way we know it. Unless the element of water becomes an integral part of *every* encounter between bodies, however seemingly irrelevant, there can never be justice.

Hydrojustice builds on an elemental reading of Spinozan ethics, where no body can flourish unless all surrounding bodies do, too.[28] This means that any position one chooses for one's body must be mediated by the ubiquitous elementality of water, which constitutes on the one hand the larger planetary body and, on the other, the movements of other bodies around, however disconnected they might appear in terms of space and time. And, further, since hydrojustice is not a goal but our actual ontological condition, in true Spinozan fashion, we have no freedom of choosing whether or not to be hydrojust. We simply *must* be, otherwise we simply *are* not, we *exist* not.

What appears as a choice, in hydrojustice is a necessity.

I would like to call this *the ethics of shared flow*. Shared flow is indeed all about freedom. But this freedom is determined immanently.

12

In my early thirties I spent most summers on a tiny Greek island of the Ionian Sea. It was so tiny that it hardly featured on the map; so remote that the only connecting boat that linked it to the bigger island did so only if the captain felt like it; so marginal that the mobile signal was mostly Albanian; and so sparsely inhabited that there was no grocery store there – and no store of any other kind. Significantly, there was only one taverna.

The freest I ever felt was there. I used to say that as soon as a second taverna opens on the island, I would stop going. Because that choice would be the end of freedom.

Freedom is inscribed in the existing flow of the body. The body flows freely but always in accordance with its movement. Immanence of movement: to act in a way that is consonant with the flows within and without. Freedom becomes a question of absence of choice.[29] Freedom is to act and not be acted upon.

Hydrojustice is immanent movement.

This means that hydrojustice gives pointers only after the body has already flowed through such pointers. Hydrojustice, being always already here, guides by confirming when the body has already moved in a direction of emergence.

This does not mean that we can relax into some sort of passive acceptance. The necessity of hydrojustice demands that humanity move away from the vertical or perish. The necessity is teleological: the various bodies *need* to flow together *in order to* keep on flowing together. If the necessity is no longer satisfied, the bodies drift apart. Human and animal bodies will bear the brunt of this drift, while Hydrogeos will most likely survive.

Let me sum up some observations, as a foretaste of the following chapters: although hydrojustice cannot be instrumentalised ('this is what we must do in order to achieve hydrojustice'), its continuous emergence can be strategised. It is a matter of *unearthing* and ceding priority to water. It is also a matter of *realigning ourselves with horizontality*, and treating even apophatic depths in a horizontal way. Hydrojustice is the politics of the aquatic *diagonal*: be water! Move like water and find your way around the surface by covering every available path in order to fulfil your thrust. Finally, it is a matter of a *palindromic* negotiation with other waters, moving between continuum and rupture in a constant manner. It is all about ebbing and flowing, confluencing and keeping separate, becoming permeable and switching to the impermeable.

In all these, the ethics of shared flow determines both the values of the apparent choice at each moment and the impossibility of choosing, if the flow is to remain free.

Wavewriting I

A Hydrojustice Manifesto

Abandon the vertical: *we desperately hang on to the vertical structures that used to define humanity, whether building up, fracking down, classifying humans and other species along pyramids of hierarchy, piling up the palimpsest of stratified detritus that covers the surface of the earth. Verticality no longer belongs to us, if it ever did: it is not even a question of abandoning verticality because of the horrors that emerged, for humanity and for the planet at large, as a result of it. Rather it is a question of understanding that this very verticality, the very element of the human upstanding, has now abandoned us. We have been dropped off the edge. Our structures are flooded.*

Embrace the horizontal: *we embrace the imposed flat, nonhierarchical ontology of the nonhuman, the aqueous continuum between the human and the bacterial, the vegetal, the insect, the animal. We swim between the material and the immaterial on one flat straight line. We cede priority to a planetary horizontality, we unearth the water from its detritus. We become a quickening of water concentration for a fraction of a breath. We accept the end of our exceptionalism and we embrace our new elementality: aquatic, gaseous, evanescently solid. Our skin no longer separates but connects. Our illusions no longer serve us. Our delusions are flattened.*

Launch the diagonal: *we do not try to float away from the horizontal. Rather, as Deleuze and Guattari urge us, we explore the diagonal as a way of remaining emplaced, nomadically constant and ready to pause the mad progress of the vertical desire. We consider the diagonal not as a solution, but as hydranecessity. We grow multiple heads that stretch across the planet, we delve into a polyamorous embrace with everything, we leak, we puddle, we rush, we coagulate. 'Most of the time, we do not see a road, but there are lots of people walking around, trying to find one. When you find a way, people follow. That is 'be water'.*[30] *We push our existence from within, conscious of our limitations, humbled by our failures. We understand that the only possible function of human exceptionalism is a responsibility to reinstate horizontality and to allow collective thriving to emerge. We all become planetary diagonals.*

2

Be Water

I

The slogan during the 2019 Hong Kong protests was taken from Hong Kong's pre-eminent fighting philosopher, actor, and thinker Bruce Lee: 'Be formless, shapeless, like water. Now you put water into a cup, it becomes the cup . . . Be water, my friend.' Faithful to water's multimodality, the protesters extended the slogan to such sayings as 'be strong like ice' when walls of water are needed to resist police force; 'be fluid like water' and spring up everywhere at once; 'gather like dew' and flash mob; 'scatter like mist' when arrest might be imminent; and 'you can't shoot water'.[1]

While metaphorical, the water of the slogan carries a physical weight. What the *Financial Times* called 'the Water Revolution' started in the rainy days of the 2014 Umbrella Revolution, with the long sit-ins and the taking over of this quintessentially maritime city in some sort of silent sirens' song. But while the Umbrella movement was mostly centralised and its leaders were easily identifiable, 'be water' had a headless fluidity, designed to avoid police arrests. The revolution has been all but quashed now, most of its leaders in prison,[2] but I am proposing to revive the slogan here, as an iteration of hydrojustice: a way of positioning one's body in relation to other bodies, together yet different, in a fluidity of choice that recalls Deleuze and Guattari's description of the game Go: rather than chess, which 'is a game of the State, or of the court: the emperor of China played it', Go 'is a question of arraying oneself in an open space, of holding space, of maintaining the possibility of springing up at any point . . . Another justice, another movement, another space-time.'[3]

This other justice, indeed hydrojustice, emerges everywhere at the same time: Hydra-like heads stretch anew every time, resilient, irrepressible, multiplying actually or virtually. They become infinite diagonals connecting the planet, a vertiginous freedom that surfs the surface of Hydrogeos. This is an amphibian justice that ushers bodies into positions of emergence, swimming in a cascade of emergencies. Belying the urgency of the situation, however, hydrojustice invites bodies to resist easy 'progress' through technological verticalities, and instead to float diffractedly in their continuum with other bodies.

Something that impressed me the first time I experienced *acqua alta* – high water – in Venice was that the water would not just spread from the banks of the canals into the city. There was no movement from the lagoon into the streets. Rather, the whole city became a strainer, allowing Hydra's multiple heads slowly but inexorably to spring out from every crack and hole on the ground. High water always starts in little puddles, an afterthought of yesterday's wave, and progressively replaces the streets with a green mesh of interconnected shallow waddling corridors. It springs all over the city almost at the same time, commanding a completely different spacetime, a much slower walking speed, a light diffracted everywhere, a soundscape of gurgles and sloshes, a city of galoshes.

2

At the time of writing, during a single week in May 2024, deadly floods hit Brazil, Kenya, Afghanistan, Tanzania, Burundi, Rwanda, and Somalia, while at the same time minor floods are ravaging various parts of the world. Flooding reports compete with droughts and impeded access to potable water, often in the same regions hit by floods. The two extremes flow together in an unsurprising paradox.[4]

Hydra: water simply needs to find its path. Valleys, low-lying cities and Pacific islands are the obvious consequences of what physicists have gently named 'communicating vessels': the water needs to balance out on a single, globe-covering surface. It has become meaningless to talk about ecological crisis any more, as Janet Roitman argues in her book *Anti-Crisis*.[5] The planet moves into fully modelled territory, the politically determined temperature rise becoming an inconvenient admission even for the radical right. Not that the environment hasn't always been dynamic and that human-induced climate change hasn't been around since at least the Industrial Revolution, as attested since the foundation of the 1988 Intergovernmental Panel on Climate Change; or that zoonotic diseases haven't impacted humanity before; or that social inequality, environmental exploitation, totalitarian regimes, or even disinformation are new occurrences. Quite the opposite: these are all part of what we have come to accept as our planetary condition.

What we are witnessing now, however, is an intensification of these processes to an unprecedented, interconnected, and urgent point. The fundamental structures, material and immaterial, on which humanity has been forming its vertical self-awareness are currently being reformulated in ways that lie beyond even our collective imagination, let alone our control. The planet is having us on a game of Go.

Hydrojustice is not about finding solutions for the water crisis – which, at a minimum, includes floods, droughts, pollution, extreme weather phenomena, and so on. Rather, hydrojustice refers to *every* issue, from geopolitical conflicts about territory through financial slumps to femicides. It is about becoming aware of the role of water in everything that occurs. Environmental humanities scholar Elizabeth DeLoughrey writes: 'if there is any agreement about climate change, it is that our planetary future is becoming more oceanic . . . producing a new sense of planetary scale and interconnectedness through the rising of a world ocean'.[6] This means that human elementality has already changed. The conceit of human exceptionalism that has determined nature ever since the Enlightenment is not something we must abandon for the sake of the planet. Rather it is something that has already abandoned us. This is Hydra's self-annihilation.

In the context of an intensification of irreversible crises, learning to deal with a future that does not include humans the way we have thought so far is hydrojustice's call to adaptation. This is what political theorist David Chandler calls 'ontopolitics of the Anthropocene': governance that gives up any attempt at knowing or anticipating issues, but focuses on adaptation.[7] Hydrojustice is less about incremental adaptation (such as more water storage, more dams, more technological solutions) and more about transformative ontological adaptation, all the way to the horizontal. In *The Water Will Come*, Jeff Goodell warns: 'despite international efforts and tireless research, there is no permanent solution – no barriers to erect or walls to build – that will protect us in the end from the drowning of the world as we know it'.[8] Verticality can no longer help us. The aquatic continuum is flooding everything.

Hydrojustice spreads low. It reminds us of the Freudian moment when humans stood upright: the consequences were shame (because one had to hide one's genitals)[9] and the compensating desire to remain 'civilised' by maintaining and augmenting that distance between the human and the ground. The higher one went, the better. But hydrojustice leaves behind vertical human supremacy, with its continuous reaching up, geyser-like – or indeed reaching down, fracking-like. There is only one shame now: the cost of our verticality. Our upstanding, all-commanding panopticon has only led us to the current anthropocenic palimpsest of detritus.

Hydrojustice invites us to rest on the surface of the water and allow a planetary jurisprudence to emerge. The new hydrohuman is a decentred, mediated, and existentially horizontal element of

Hydrogeos that deals with the vulnerabilities of other bodies without encroaching upon them.

We need to rediscover our horizontality.

3

Hydrojustice, more than ecojustice, climate justice, or other green understandings of justice, and certainly more than any anthropic concept of justice, is our best way to capture the current predicament and imagine a way forward.

Hydrojustice is not distributive (it is not concerned with water as a resource), procedural (it is not about fairness in the legal sense of the word), or restorative (it does not deal for example with environmental reparations). Hydrojustice is a material and metaphorical reality that is already here (as opposed to the Derridean justice perpetually to arrive, *à venir*, a messianic promise), ferociously emplaced yet moving (as opposed to the Rawlsian veiled and fair equality of opportunity), fully embodied (as opposed to most phenomenological accounts of just human consciousness). It does not provide a solution but only a direction, a call to continuous repositioning and adaptation on all fronts (political, psychological, material). It works along Deleuzian lines of flight, Glissantian archipelagic thought, and Spinozan ethical placement: it is an immanent flow.

And that's the challenge, since the paradox of hydrojustice requires constant flow between its sides. Here is an example: hydrojustice cannot be inscribed within the barren debate between anthropocentrism and ecocentrism. As Astrida Neimanis writes, 'there is no border where water ends and culture begins; where non-human bodies of water stop and human bodies of water take up; where natural forces rule and humans submit or where human culture rules and nature submits. Water is eminently naturalcultural.'[10]

Rather, hydrojustice places itself on another, more generative paradox: that between continuum and rupture. To take the continuum first: we are all bodies of water, as Neimanis, Alaimo, and other hydrofeminist thinkers tell us. Even further, we are all part of this vast water body. Let's imagine Spinoza as the greatest hydrotheorist who famously subsumed all bodies to god or nature – or Mami Wata, Tipua, Poseidon, Oshun, Ra. Every body (human and nonhuman, animate and inanimate, material and immaterial) is part of the great aquatic substance. Yet every body takes on a form: 'water needs a body – it needs to take up expression as bodies of water that are specifically situated, even in all of their porous transits'.[11] These bodies of water, however, like Hydra's heads sprouting from within one another, are constantly communicating, leaking, perspiring, bleeding into all the other bodies of water; even the image of the drowned immigrant, a blanket over their body as a gesture of belated hospitality – as geopolitics theorist Joseph Pugliese writes in his take on bodies of water – bleeds across the media, carrying across that 'soft death of water, soft death after the violence of flailing arms and hands clasping the nothing of water'.[12] All bodies bleed into one another.

Where, then, can one place the limit between water and world, since all world is water?[13] Not outside. There is no outside, sings Zarathustra. The outside is inside, between the waves of the planet. The limit turns inward, becomes a fold. It does not disappear, but it loses its outside.

If the whole world is water, then the whole world becomes a limit.

And here comes rupture. I understand rupture not just as the difference between an individual body of water and the larger continuum, nor just as the difference of identity between the various bodies of water. Rather, rupture is the folding of the continuum in waves of repetition, each repetition a new, unique moment of difference, a wave on the surface of Hydrogeos, a cosmogonic echo of aquatic origin and finality. Here's Carribean thinker Edouard Glissant's archipelagic thought: 'The whole world is becoming an archipelago and creolising.'[14] No single root, just distances between island worlds, swept up by a repeated historical process of creolisation: an inevitable wave of multiplicity and 'unpredictability, ambiguity, fragility, drift . . . rerouting'[15] that augurs a new way of both belonging to a particular space and connecting to the rest of the world.

There is no hierarchy in the paradox between continuum and rupture. Both are part of this grand aquatic surface that has no outside. It all plays out on the ontological flatness that extends through all bodies, animate and inanimate alike. This does not mean, however, that all bodies are equally strong – and this is indeed the difference from a Latourian flat ontology. Rather the surface is tilted, given to a human verticality that determines all other bodies: stronger, more able, better situated, privileged, wealthier bodies push the surface down and all bodies of water eddy around that depression. The state of the planet is precisely this verticality: continuous capitalist investment on fossil fuels, extractive economy, enduring colonialism and exploitation, intrahuman and environmental violence. Verticality has become untenable.

Understanding the mechanics of this paradox, as I try to do in this book, helps us to recognise our current predicament as the loss of our (false) exceptionalism. The rupture of the aquatic continuum can no longer be seen as human supremacy.

We allow ourselves finally to lie in the low waters that cover the globe.

4

In one of the most celebrated scenes of Hayao Miyazaki's *Spirited Away*, the protagonist accompanied by a ghost rides a train on shallow waters. The ghost, evanescent and translucent, still leaks the warm vaporous liquidity of the Onsen bath they just left behind, its mist bleeding into the whole scene. The train is bound to what is essentially the safe fantasy of a cottage deep in a night forest. The surrounding water is low, as if the whole planet had been replaced by a lake.

Through the train windows we see stations whistling by steeped in water, lapping wavelets tending to the rail lines, a quiet dusk mirrored on every surface. We look at the two passengers looking out. We also look through the train window and let the water surface to seep into the carriage. Our position is privileged: flowing between the inside and the outside, between the two sides of the window.

This is the placement of hydrojustice: not a homeostasis but a constant shift of perspectives, from the water to the human to the 'natural' to the 'inanimate' and so on, in order to carry on adjusting to the changing conditions. Hydrojustice is a window through which we see ourselves seeing, sensing, flowing. And water is our medium: the conduit to a deep affective state, prior to walking or even crawling, an amniotic sliding along the womb of the world.

The elementality of water cannot be contained in a list of its physical qualities. Water's relevance is mainly manifested in its ability to connect bodies, times, and spaces. Water gives rise to a set of affects, namely informational, sensorial, and emotional stimuli that set the scene for life and death for whole communities, regions, and continents. As Renita Holmes, a Miami resident suffering as a result of water rising, says, '[s]ea level is about me'.[16] There can never be an absence of aquatic affects, be it in the memory of wells, the writing of rivers across geology, the end of ice, the mist of industry, the bloating seas, or the promiscuity of leaking bodies. The whole gamut of affects, from joy to joylessness, connects water to the world.

For Carl Jung, water is the symbolic locus of the unconscious,[17] the *participation mystique* for all beings. Every waterbody is connected to the collective unconscious, that vast reservoir of the world that Jung introduced into contemporary psychoanalysis. Be water! And the world is mirrored on the water's surface and sees itself beyond any mask or persona. The depth surges, becomes surface, and we are all facing it.

5

All bodies use water as an affective conduit, to transfer other bodies, emotions, and meaning.

Water is an avenue of communication and transport, whether in charting a trade route, finding a safe space from a hunt, or spreading nutrients, information, and care through mycelia. Affects are contagious, as feminist psychoanalyst Teresa Brennan shows;[18] they rush like spring torrents on a valley and take over spaces and bodies.

Affects move especially fast if spaces are confined, if bodies lie next to one another, water is everywhere, and there is nowhere for these bodies to go. In late June 2023, a nameless boat (subsequently understood to have been named *Adriana*), bound for Europe and carrying more than 700 immigrants from Egypt, sank. More than 600 people drowned. This, one of the greatest tragedies in the Mediterranean, was almost entirely eclipsed by another incident that happened in the same week: the *Titan* submersible – a state-of-the-art vessel especially designed for an experimental but supposedly safe expedition to the depths of the Atlantic, to view the wreck of the *Titanic* – imploded, killing all five men onboard.

There is no doubt that both incidents were horrific. Yet note the verticality in action: the world got disproportionately mobilised as a result of a media frenzy that fed on the enduring allure of the *Titanic*, the doomed glamour of the submersible, and of course the xenophobia that accompanies every migrant crossing. Millions of dollars were spent on *Titan*'s rescue efforts, and we got to know everything about the five men onboard. Meanwhile, the Egyptian migrant boat case turned into a bitter exchange of accusations between the eastern Mediterranean governments involved – Greece, Italy, and Malta – concerning their responsibility in saving the immigrants. After an examination of the conditions of the shipwreck, the European Ombudsman found that Frontex, the border agency, had, arguably, limited powers to go against explicit requests by a member state (in this case, Greece) not to intervene.[19] It was an all-round failure, possibly even with criminal intent, which confirms the absurd verticality of national politics and of various mediation bodies that purposefully block any sense of responsibility for suffering.

The migrant ship was one of hundreds of rickety boats that cross the Mediterranean every year, filled to the brim with desperate people from the global South. Hydrojustice reminds us that this is no longer simply a passing refugee crisis, but an inexorable predicament that keeps on pushing us to verticalities we no longer desire or are able to manage. Even on the most optimistic scenarios, climatic conditions are changing so rapidly that climate refugees, including from southern into sacrosanct northern Europe, will become the norm.[20]

There is no outside. There is only water, and this is where every body starts and ends.

6

The infamous diagrams of slave ships with abducted Africans 'rationally' distributed in the ship's hull folded in the ocean give us the vaguest indication of an enduring horror.

There are no windows. We are not even allowed the luxury of imagining an outside. In this 'womb abyss', as Glissant calls it,[21] there is only the apophatic terror of the inside. The 'cargo' was moved up, near the windows, only when it was to be thrown. This is just one of many Black Atlantic stories of murdered Africans, but one that has endured because of the 1783 court case of *Gregson v Gilbert*, where the ship's owners (Gregson) took to court the underwriters (Gilbert) for the insurance value of the murdered cargo. Water is present in various guises in this story, but most intriguingly as rainfall that enabled the crew to replenish their water provisions. But provisions were not a decision-making factor, as Black studies theorist Christina Sharpe writes when retelling the story of the *Zong*.[22] 'Upon the evidence, there appears to have been no necessity' to throw overboard 130 people, as judge Lord Mansfield observed.[23]

A different water, however, has been added to this driest, brutal law case. M. NourbeSe Philip, in her book-long poem and performance piece *Zong!*, carves deep gaps among the words of the legal document,[24] rearranges them into gashes and apertures so that water can flow in between, open up the silence of the bodies, and give them back to water. These legal pauses create space for a mirroring of law's violent limitations: the law 'regretted'[25] that the abducted Africans were considered cargo, mere property, as animals or machines are considered now. But the case was simply an insurance claim case, not a murder case. In the watery pauses between the rearranged case words, we are forced to face the law's inadequacy.

Hydrojustice can use the law: it is sometimes the best way to shift obstinate verticalities. Justice in general is often linked to the legal process. But one must not be lulled into a false security. In deciding the *Gregson v Gilbert* case, the court was acting according to the law of the time. Sticking to the law is not a guarantee for justice. Sticking to the law often goes against hydrojustice. In *Gregson v Gilbert* there was no justice in place, just law.

One of the videos from the performances of *Zong!* on the author's website ends with three women filmed from the back, hauntingly standing in shallow waters, holding hands and looking out towards a watery horizon. These women seem at home in a slow horizontality, their bodies in communion with the water in and around them.

This is hydrojustice: separate bodies that hold one another close; a moment of immersion in the watery present, a rebaptising of the past – but also a moment of no confrontation, no juridical adversarialism, no Levinasian facing of the face of the other. Sliding needs no face, no facing or face-off. Sliding relies on Glissantian *opacity*, namely the ethical responsibility of never fully knowing the other.[26] Hydrojustice means: a shift from seeing an other (with the discriminatory tendencies that come with it) to sensing or feeling the other and their inherent unknowability.[27]

7

There are two emergences of hydrojustice amid the horror of the ship, not revealed in the organisational solidity of the cargo plan: first, the leaking bodies of the abducted Africans, who fill the space between them with a continuous affective transfer of wet breaths, sweat, blood, piss, and tears, but also sperm and vaginal fluids running across every combination of gender and race. This was taking place both between the chained male bodies and between the often unchained female bodies – unchained, so that they may be within easy reach of the sailors, but also mobile and claiming an aquatic agency: 'surrounded by churning, unseen waters, these brutalized bodies themselves became liquid, oozing', as Omise'eke Natasha Tinsley discovers in her historical research on queer sexualities of the Caribbean.[28]

And, second, apart from the 130 or so men and women who were violently jettisoned into the ocean, ten of the captured men jumped into the water by themselves, presumably while the murders were taking place. One could never really imagine this to have been of their own volition. They were not faced with a choice between different life courses. This exuberant moment of agency needs to be placed in its full hydrophobic context: most of the abducted Africans were terrified of the open sea. In the words of Olaudah Equiano just before he was pushed onboard the ship, 'I had never before seen any water larger than a pond or a rivulet, and my surprise was . . . soon converted to terror'.[29]

Yet there is a chilling sense of freedom in the actions of both the erotic and the suicidal bodies: an arch of decision to leave behind, even momentarily, even orgasmically, any present horror and future misery, and launch themselves in the possibility of other waters, waters near them and waters below them: 'fluid black bodies refusing to accept that the liquidation of their social selves – the colonization of oceanic and body waters – meant the liquidation of their sentient selves'.[30]

I would like to think of these divers unto eros and divers unto thanatos as pulsating instances of hydrojustice. A justice of horizontality, where the body of water bridges its distance with the vast continuum. 'Where is the dialectic? In the sea', as the *quilombola* thinker Beatriz Nascimento writes.[31] In horror and fear puddles the body of water that harbours this world's dialectics: 'the Atlantic as a free and physical territory made meetings and unmeetings of disparate Cultures possible. Both genocides and genetic transformations.'

Be water: become one with one's deepest fear of death.

Be water: become one with one's deepest desire for death.

8

In July 2019 I was invited to give a performance at the Royal Danish Cast Collection in Copenhagen[32] – a quirky assemblage of stucco reproductions of the whole western sculptural canon, reinterpreted in pristine whitewashed sensuality.

During my research and talks with the collection director Henrik Holm, a hidden empire story emerged. The building, a multistorey warehouse-like red-brick structure overlooking the port, was the seat of the Danish slave trade, administered by the Danish East India Company. The top floor hosts the gilded council room and a series of strategically placed windows: a vertical panopticon overseeing all port transactions. An estimated 120,000 captured Africans were transferred from western Africa to the Danish colonies on Virgin Islands, to work on the plantations.[33]

The port's water floods the baroque council room and gushes all the way down the floors below. Porous white statues float around us. It is still the case that the Danish colonial past remains largely unacknowledged.[34]

The hall becomes a slave ship, the audience the human cargo, and I, the performer, become the ghost of a captain that leaks guilt. I come out of my hiding station, where I performed a text about our traumas and complicity. The place of my voice is now taken by the soundscape that the artist Julie Nymann has created.[35] There are waters churning in that soundscape, openness violently rushing into small enclosures, a raging ocean, creaking floorboards, a solid aural materiality that conjures the ineffable. I walk through the orderly cargo, previously arranged by the evening's assistants: its members are positioned in rows facing each other, reproducing the slave ship map. Their wrists are tied up in pairs with those of the person standing next to them, to make sure that they all stay put despite the waves, the dead bodies among them, the soaking seawater, the rats, the putrefaction.

An average 32 per cent of the enslaved Africans die during the three months' journey.[36] The ghost of the ship's captain walks among the living ones and places a black dot on the forehead of 32 per cent of the participants, about sixty people. The remaining 120 or so are fed fresh strawberries. Their skin must look glossy upon arrival: the better they look, the higher the price.[37]

The sixty people, mainly white middle-class Copenhageners, are touched by the ghost (the title I chose for the performance) with random dots of infinitesimal deaths. Something is whispered in their ear, *forgive me* perhaps, or was it *remember me*, the sound of the crashing waves is too booming, one cannot hear well. My whispering gets drowned in the vast matter of early capitalist putrefaction.

9

Every performance has a pivot, around which the whole edifice revolves.

I reach a Black woman, one of the few in the audience. She is not tied up to her neighbour. I feel that she sees into me, my despair to do the right thing, me, a white privileged man, who also holds the privilege of the stage right there. My urge is to spare her, to allow her to die now, before the worst comes, before she reaches the colonies and is put to slow death through labour, an act of kindness I thought, but who am I to decide, how can I raise my arm, the black of the paint pouring from the roof of the Royal Cast Collection, its regal, white, collected, perfectly unoriginal perfect gypsum, who am I, but the ghost raises my arm anyway to mark her with the black dot, and she mouths, no, she shakes her head, no, but she does not move away, she remains fierce, filled with a tremendous agency, looking at me, I am wavering but I press on, I incline towards her ear, I'll try to give her the utterance now, please listen, forgive me, forgive him, forgive me, forgive us.

And she says no. She motions me with her

hand, go away, move to the next one. I am not here to forgive you.

Be water, she did. Her water was steadfast, a wall of liquidity that would not budge, confronting the ghost, her resistance an arch of proud self-determination amid the trauma. The time has not yet come for us to move. The water needs to soak the planet for longer, till we manage to invite our ghosts past and present to sit with us on the table.

After the performance I caught up with her, to see how she was and to thank her. Astonishingly, she apologised for not playing along. The only thing I could do after that was to apologise again and to thank her precisely for that: for her not 'playing along'.

Wavewriting II

Mediation

Your hand glided away from mine. We drifted apart. You somewhere else, me somewhere here, both bodies suspended mid-water, volumes of water above and below us in that gigantic baptismal urn, resigned to our ever-departing past.

I looked for you but the water had taken you across the atrium. Your eyes were shut, you looked as if you were in a trance.

Our connection was mediated by something much bigger than either of us. It was as if we had found something that was the other for each other, a floating calm that sheltered us from harshness, a refuge of breathlessness. I let my eyes shut too, finding a drop of breath in me and spreading it through my body.

. . .

We were pushed and pulled by what felt like an invisible crowd, translucent bodies whose contour was barely discernible, heavenly bodies that ignored us, shoving us aside and in the process making us spin around ourselves like dying goldfish.

But despite the violence of that pull, it felt like a return.

For a brief moment, we became part of a multiplicity, one drop among thousands of oceans, one breath exhaled in the aether – but we had finally, however briefly, however temporarily, however perhaps randomly, stopped being mere observers. We had become part of it. The violence was pure, the thrust primordial, the speed terrifying, and even our separation from each other felt complete and almost final. But in losing each other in the water, we found a different each other. Perhaps for the first time, we really found each other.

We were dying a new life.[38]

3

Water in Water

I

Where does water end?

I owe Georges Bataille the poetic formulation of the chapter's title: 'An atom of nitrogen, of gold, or a molecule of water exist without needing anything from what surrounds them; they remain in a state of perfect immanence ... like water in water'.[1]

In this chapter I focus on the continuum between bodies of water. As Astrida Neimanis writes, 'we are bodies of water... we are not on the one hand embodied (with all of the cultural and metaphysical investments of this concept) while on the other hand primarily comprising water (with all of the attendant biological, chemical, and ecological implications). We are both of these things, inextricably and at once.'[2] Embodiment is watery: this means that it is on the one hand a momentary containment, namely a discursive snapshot of corporeal autonomy and an epistemological tool for identifying (self, others, movement); and on the other a continuous affirmation of dispersion, of being always other, of never managing to establish an outside (or an inside). Watery embodiment is the grand subsumption of the difference between immanence and transcendence into one vast, turbulent continuum.

Continuum is one aspect of the paradox of hydrojustice, one artificially separated side of the fold with rupture. By focusing on continuum in this chapter I choose to deal with an important aspect of hydrojustice: its immanence. An immanent hydrojustice means that everything in the continuum between bodies is mediated by water and that any encounter in space and time between bodies implicates water.

'Water in water': the signifier of the aquatic continuum.

2

I have always been drawn to water. To this day, my art practice and my fiction writing are driven by a curiosity for the way water looks and feels; and by awe for how it could transform me and everything around me into a permanent indefiniteness of form.

I hesitantly place the conscious beginning of this fascination at an encounter in my father's summer house in Greece when I was twelve years old. For context, my summers were generally quite lonely. I wasn't especially confident around the neighbourhood kids. I was an interloper, only occasionally spending time at the summer house. In many ways I felt disembodied from what I thought my self was supposed to be. I felt at a distance, observing myself rather than living me. And in that sense, I often felt in communion with the outside. Late afternoons usually found me swimming alone, not in particularly deep waters but deep enough to make me panic if something were to happen. Much later, I read about Shelley's apparently famous death wish by water.

His attraction to it was so overwhelming that it would push him to extremes, although his aquatic desire 'was matched only by his disinclination to make any attempt to stay afloat in it'.[3] Shelley eventually drowned on the coast in central Italy, a culmination of his love for the element.

On that particular afternoon, the sea was calm, its surface a deep pine green reflecting the mountain slope around the beach. Suddenly, as if from within this reflected image, trees and rocks part and an enormous jellyfish emerges, larger than me, holding space in an imperious indifference, radiating a kind of magnetic slowness around it.

Fear, awe and a fair bit of trembling took over, a distinctly Kierkegaardian moment of continuum with something vast. Neither the jellyfish nor I were budging from the space. Not unlike Shelley, I was barely able to stay afloat, let alone swim away. I was holding my breath, turning slightly away so that I wouldn't give out any confrontation vibes, but my peripheral vision fixed on its movement in fear and also mad curiosity. The jellyfish, on the other hand, was majestically moving its tentacles until I felt I was moving along the rhythm it was dictating, almost like a pulse.

While I have never consciously had the same aquatic death drive as Shelley, I have been able to sympathise with an Ophelia-like abandon to the water. I have always been fascinated (not without distress, of course) by the idea of becoming finally entangled with the vast interiority of the outside, taking part in the misty correspondence between immanence and transcendence, losing myself in bubbly particles.

There was a period I was obsessed with jellyfish in my painting practice. They would appear everywhere, bodies of transparency on canvas, cardboard or wood. But the self-imposed, hard principle was always this: never add any extra paint to the canvas. Jellyfish should always emerge from within, an immanent form that would evolve from the priming or the paint I had already applied on the surface. Scrap and grind, dilute and reduce whatever material was already there, until the form of the jellyfish emerges. I was moving my hand but it often felt like I was merely following the movements of the yet-to-emerge form. Water in water. I was always confident that I would find the jellyfish exactly where I was looking for it.

That first encounter with the jellyfish was an early taste of the continuum.

3

Jellyfish, Stacy Alaimo writes, are 'barely distinct from the seas that surround them, existing as flowing, pulsing, gelatinous, and just barely organized bodies. Jellies somehow live as the very element that surrounds them.'[4] This is not just an impression but factually true. Jellyfish have a very low biomass, with more than 95 per cent of their body just water molecules, which makes their density very similar to that of seawater.[5] Their transparency, so absolute that satellites cannot monitor them,[6] allows us to think of them as simple extensions of the water around them, random encapsulations, gossamer insides in a world without outside.

Jellyfish exemplify the continuum between body and planet, one body of water nestled in another, vast body of water. They 'question the humanist desire for solid demarcations. With their apparent yet unfathomable "lack" of an inside, jellies may entice us into posthumanist states of wonder.'[7] They are as close as possible to being water in water, immanence within immanence, a double immanence folded, coiled in, ensconced. They challenge appearances of individual forms and point towards their continuum with the body beyond them. They embody the perfect immanence: their mouth is also their excretory orifice.

There is, however, violence in this folding. In Bataille, the quintessence of water in water, namely of animal immanence, is animal eating animal. For immanence is also one body disappearing in another, water becoming other water. Violence is part of the continuum, a turbulence generated during the negotiations between bodies of water. Interestingly, food shortage might push jellyfish to this ultimate expression of immanence: eat one another. The softness is belied.

But there is a difference between a violence that comes from above, parsed out as a means to meaningless power (what Bataille would call transcendental violence), and an immanent violence that takes place between bodies, at the level of molecules, where life and death happen.

This is the difference that allows us to speak of hydrojustice.

To recall Deleuze, there is a justice 'that is opposed to all judgment, according to which bodies are marked by each other, and the debt is inscribed directly on the body'.[8] This is the horizontality of hydrojustice. No divine judgement, no punishing deluge – just bodies moving along one another, and in the process marking one another. This is the horizontality of every interaction. And traversing it is the diagonal of hydrojustice: cutting across species, eras, spaces, and connecting it with water even when water is not apparent or seemingly relevant. Diagonal hydrojustice brings forth the aquatic continuum.

4

Jellyfish proliferate in the Anthropocene: what is a difficult, often lethal environment for most other species (humans included) works in favour of the jellyfish. Jellyfish blooms are the product of our hyper-industrialisation: this is an anthropocenic animal if there ever was one, flourishing in effluence. Geographer Elizabeth R. Johnson writes: 'low-oxygen, high-acidity environments and warmer ocean temperatures also seem to be well suited to jellyfish life. Anoxic and hypoxic areas – the "dead zones" that grow off our coasts as a result of excessive fertilizer runoff from the land – suffocate most living marine organisms. Jellyfish, however, absorb and store oxygen in their gelatinous bell.'[9] In yet another show of immanence, jellyfish contain their life environment within, even though their 'transparency allows us to literally see through them so that there is no "inside". Jellies "pull the 'outside' waters within"',[10] allowing the continuum to give them life.

Water in water: jellyfish become coextensive with their surrounding water, blur the boundaries between bodies, nestle into warm pollution and create a peculiar maritime predominance, since their predators, succumbing to environmental degradation, are becoming fewer and fewer. The continuum, in other words, is a tool of survival. The body internalises its outside, tames it, as it were, while being tamed by it. The affect circulates both ways and ties the bodies in closer communion, beyond judgement. 'A shared ontological principle', writes literary ocean scholar Edwige Tamalet Talbayev, 'water enacts continuity and kinship across categories of life.'[11]

The ambiguous moral message of the jellyfish is what we are currently facing: yes, we can and must prevent, and even reverse, environmental degradation. But hydrojustice is not nostalgia for a world that no longer exists. We cannot but accept this toxicity as our current predicament and save what we can, while reconfiguring both humanity and its connections to Hydrogeos.

When in danger, jellyfish can revert from its mature to its polyp stage, becoming potentially immortal. The planet's ontological condition is that of the jellyfish: a conative force at any cost. Jellyfish is perhaps the lifeform closest to hydrojustice.

This means that hydrojustice might entail a (self-)obliteration of humanity.

5

Science historian Steven Shapin writes: 'There's an old joke that London tap water has been through seven kidneys before it reaches your lips – but the real number of historical kidneys is probably orders of magnitude larger. We're all connected . . . The water supply links everybody's kidneys to everybody's lips.'[12] Continuum does not presuppose a continuity of the same form. Rather, it is about transformation. Just like water's continual cycle from solid to liquid to gas and back again, bodies in the hydrocontinuum move in the same way between forms, momentarily quickening into recognisable shapes or dissolving into vastness. Causalities between forms get frozen or vapourised, passages become dammed up or rushed down, temporalities arch along planetary routes or minuscule eternities.

Continuum means passage.

Perhaps no one has put it as beautifully as Neimanis:

> Bodies of water puddle and pool. They seek confluence. They flow into one another in life-giving ways, but also in unwelcome, or unstoppable, incursions. Even in an obstinate stagnancy they slowly seep and leak. We owe our own bodies of water to others, in both dribbles and deluges. These bodies are different – in their physical properties and hybridizations, as well as in political, cultural, and historical terms – but their differing from one another, their differentiation, is a collective worlding.[13]

Collective worlding is not just a matter of common creation but one of collective positioning of the bodies that make up this flowing world. A triple positioning: first, in relation to the continuum with Hydrogeos, the body of water of which all bodies are part, the one immanence that floats in its very own waters; second, in relation to the continuum of the forms that every body takes over time; and, third, in relation to other bodies.

6

The first continuum, the one between body and Hydrogeos, means that all floating and sliding of bodies in relation to one another, all pause and movement, are mediated by the aquatic vastness of which they are part. This means that *every* intra-action between bodies is with and about water, a sort of elemental triangulation: intra-action as the internal workings of the elemental.

This has far-reaching consequences for law and politics: if all bodies are water bodies and all the space between them is water, then how can law and politics, which are about the movement of bodies in space in relation to other bodies, ignore water? Water cannot be just a symbol for the state of the earth, a thing to recall when there's too much or too little of it, or a glib addendum to the thought process of environmental legal or political argumentation.

Rather no transaction, negotiation, or partnership should be able to take place without due consideration to water.

Western law of course has always worked at the level of forms – that is, legally identifiable, discreet units of legal capacity that interact with similar forms. While water is included, indeed embodied in these forms, the law cannot and perhaps does not want to acknowledge it. Waters 'resist inscription'[14] and law cannot operate unless it inscribes, categorises, simplifies, defines, distinguishes, fixes. Its individualism is paramount in matters of property – it is, arguably, the main driving force of western law. Even in Roman law when a thing was held in common by all (*res omnium communis*), water involved property conflict in delectable ways: the word 'rival' originates in the Latin word *rivalis*, which meant person who shares the same brook or canal (and, by extension, neighbourhood).[15]

Law is not alone in this. The western conceptual edifice is based on a hardcore version of anthropocentric individualism. Neimanis writes: 'while anthropocentrism privileges human bodies over non-human ones, individualism refuses to see that human bodies are also riven through, sustained, composed of, and produced by non-human bodies of water as well – rendering the notion of the individual a poor fit with aqueous ontologies and ecologies'.[16] Yet most of the current discussions focus on precisely that or, at most, on an extended version of that. When we think of law and water, indeed of hydrojustice, we often think of distributive justice with reference to water as a resource; we think, namely, of access to water and rights to water. We might possibly think of rights of the water bodies themselves, as it happened in national jurisdictions across the globe when rivers and lakes were at stake.

As mentioned earlier, there is no doubt that these elements are important – as mobilising and awareness-raising discussions as well as on their own, as legal and political successes. But this is merely a basic achievement, which ultimately fails to address the vast challenges Hydrogeos is facing. Law needs to eddy around a radical consideration of water as an omnipresent juridical and political factor.

7

'The law has all but moved into the unavoidable foreground, making the water in front of us a matter of law first and foremost, blessing and transforming the waters into a mere instance of what we might call legal waters, or waters of the law,'[17] as religious studies scholar Gil Anidjar writes about the almost sacred responsibility of the law towards water.

The law must become water.

Such a consistent mediation, in law, of something other than a (rational, individualistic, human) way of thinking is not an oddity. Many jurisprudential traditions practise this, from Confucian-inflected collectivity, through Islamic divine mediation, to indigenous juridical cosmogonies. In the secular sphere, simply living in regions that, either traditionally or because of climate change, are challenged by rising waters and by droughts shows how hydrojustice – in the sense of water mediation in every intra-action between bodies – is not a preference but a reality we need to adapt to. In Venice, Barbara Casavecchia writes, 'to live next to/with a lagoon also means to learn to think with tides, moons, climate emergencies, water levels rising, sea and fog, and interconnected ecosystems where very little stands still'.[18] The defences are limited and temporary in view of the continuously rising waters. Venetians have traditionally used metal sheets on their front doors to protect themselves from high tide – a technique also used in the Netherlands that Mikki Stelder finds nevertheless to be a dispositive of juridical limitation rather than an efficient tool: 'there are limitations to capturing and juridicalizing the water. The blue planet speaks back to regimes of property and capture – it speaks through rising sea levels and ocean acidification.'[19] Even so, these metal surfaces remain the enduring negotiator between bodies of water.

Similarly, in places like Miami, sea risings and storms mean that previously undesirable and for this reason affordable areas such as Little Haiti are becoming the new investment haunt, on account of their higher ground away from the surf. The BBC reported on this climate gentrification, which disproportionately affects the non-white, non-male, lower income residents, under the eloquent title 'When Sea Levels Rise, So Does Your Rent'.[20] Of course, the porous limestone ground underneath Little Haiti only temporarily protects from the water, which, like in Venice and everywhere perennially soaked, 'comes from the bottom, not just from the side'.[21]

Water as property means: we only save what counts for western-determined verticality.

8

The second continuum, that between the forms that every body takes, is a continuum of temporality. It has to do with the way water affects the history and the future of a body and its relation to its desire both for returning and for expanding and flowing elsewhere.

Art curator Ovul Durmusoglu wonders: 'is it possible that one always desires to return to the sea that formed the essence of one's blood systems? The sea that became the minerals of one's body?'[22] And just as one wants to return and even regress into the amnion of the past, in the same way water itself exercises a mnemonic agency for its own need to return. Toni Morrison's words on the Mississippi river are instructive: '"floods" is the word they use, but in fact it is not flooding; it is remembering. Remembering where it used to be. All water has a perfect memory and is forever trying to get back to where it was.'[23]

Return is always also a departure: a perfect repetition is neither possible nor desirable. Return means returning to water always as difference, the same waters anew, Heraclitus reiterated every time, a series of differences to the *n*th Deleuzian power,[24] which never reproduces the original difference. Let's think of it as spiral passage, a Moebius circularity that extends ad infinitum and haunts molecules, organs, foetuses, gods, ghosts.

Those drowned in the sea become what Tamalet Talbayev calls 'residual ontologies: dehumanized bodies that fall prey to dissolution and dispersal under the combined power of corrosive seawater, marine sea life, tides, and currents'.[25] The Black Atlantic becomes the locus of fertile divinities, dissipation moving towards eternal return. Artist Ayesha Hameed speaks of mineralisation: 'solids turning to salinity as bones turn to calcium, and vice versa. This is the temporalization of organic matter becoming inorganic and flipping back again.'[26] And, I would add, the temporalisation of all forms taken by a body of water, a flipping back and an unfolding forward, retaining a memory of adaptability and resistance.

'Water overflows with memory', writes Caribbean theorist M. Jacqui Alexander. 'Emotional memory. Bodily memory. Sacred memory.'[27] Water molecules, our own water bodies, carry the affective loads of past and future. Water memory is persistent, geological, and corporeal in one vast arch. It is all here: 'water holds in it a past as remote as that gaseous primordial soup, as well as a future, unforeseeable'.[28] Cultural theorist Janine MacLeod writes: 'The material memory of water . . . is not only retentive; it is also communicative.'[29] Water extends into the past as memory, into the present as communication, into the future as return. Aquatic temporality is always multiple, differentiated, unreproducible. Yet, like Hydra's heads, these pasts and futures never cease being part of the larger water body.

The consequences for hydrojustice are decisive. Encompassing past and future constellations of a body in an attempt to understand the just positioning of bodies in, and in relation to, water is an extraordinarily complex endeavour. Even initiatives such as strict liability, where the link between climate change and specific human actions is assumed, are merely timid steps towards a more horizontal understanding of responsibility and, eventually, towards a more liquid law.[30] But the challenge of the continuum is much larger.

'Aquatic continuum' means that all bodies of water are all *other* bodies of water, simultaneously or at some point in their past or future.

We can learn from indigenous relationality: 'all people or beings are better understood as the embodiment of all the beings in their relational orbit that have, are and have previously come *[sic]* before them'.[31] There can be no otherness in water. The temporal circularity of every body of water and its forms means that, at some point in its cycle of matter (because here we also talk about inanimate bodies), all bodies of water have contributed to its movement.

Politically, this implies a diffused complicity, a shared but differentiated level of guilt, an agonising burden of responsibility for all bodies. Naturally some bodies are more instrumental than others in committing violence. This is the still omnipresent verticality that dislocates our flatness. But political, geochemical, geographical, or historical causalities are often unprovable. This is not about allowing actors to 'get away with it'. Rather, it is about understanding that traditional conceptualisations of justice as retribution are not relevant any more.

Hydrogeos cannot wait. It is flattening out along with us, in ways that any return might eventually exclude us.

9

Continuum is hydrojustice.

On the one hand, the obligatory legal and political mediation of water in all conflicts and confluences renders hydrojustice a fluid that is everywhere and that informs every foreground consideration. On the other, awareness of the circularity of the return renders hydrojustice a molecular emergence, always present materially in every movement of bodies across time.

Hydrojustice is continuum.

Pure immanence, no outside, all circularity, constantly present in whatever movement takes place; fully immanent ('there is no outside') and, at the same time, fully Nietzschean ('there is no outside! But we forget. How wonderful it is that we forget'):[32] an artificial, illusionary but ultimately necessary transcendence is right here, on the surface of Hydrogeos. It goes nowhere else (where else could it go?) but opens up oceans of breath within lakes of enclosure. And that often seems to be enough for the planet to carry on.

10

In early 2024, an exoplanet seventy light years away was discovered with a chemical mix consistent with a water world. Water would span the entire surface of this planet, which has twice the radius of the Earth and a temperature of at least 100 degrees Celsius.[33] Scientists have been debating whether at such high temperatures water can be liquid or becomes a thick soup, in a zone of indistinction between liquid and gas.

This discovery runs parallel to something that science has known for a while now: that there is water suspended between planets and even between galaxies, moving along like clouds on the sky.[34] The latest discovery, in 2023, revealed a 12-billion-year-old body of water around a feeding black hole.[35]

Marine celestial phenomena are relatively frequent occurrences. But we also know that there are water reservoirs at the core of our planet, as inaccessible as outer space reservoirs. Although the water is split and its chemical ingredients are bound up in rock formations, these are considered actual water reservoirs at the core of Hydrogeos. According to what is widely accepted as a solid scientific hypothesis, water arrived on Earth in rock formations, from space, subsequently seeping below the surface and creating those inner earth reservoirs.[36]

Science meets cosmogonies. In most of the ancient creation myths, from the Yazidis through the Greeks to the Aboriginals, the world emerges from the midst of a cosmic sea. Water is the womb of the world, be it the world of diver gods in Native American lore or that of ritual fishing on the islands of Polynesia. This vector appears in one of the first sentences of the Jewish and Christian Genesis (1: 6–8). On day one of creation, God separates water from water: there is a water above and a water below, in the middle of which he places the firmament. According to some theological interpretations, these are angels and demons, for there was no physical water until day six of creation. According to others, there is nothing allegorical about it: the division is between waters on earth and waters in gaseous form in the sky. As the early Christian theologian Basilius Magnus (Basil of Caesarea) says, 'let water be water'.[37]

A most vertiginous continuum emerges between outer and inner waters, a vector surface that links them up in an immanence unafraid of distance, difference, the passing of time: like water in water, where all waters have been, or will be at some point, part of all other waters; a continuum that accommodates distance, indeed rupture of the very continuum, without ever being tilted into desperate verticality.

Thought of like this, cosmically and cosmogonically, extending even beyond Hydrogeos, hydrojustice becomes, properly speaking, a cosmic emergence.

Wavewriting III

'Go to the Water' Ritual

amó:hi   atsv:sdi
water place   to go and return

*Now! Listen! Long Man,[38] very quickly You have
    just come to hear,*
*You who took Your origin from the water-
    seep:*
very quickly You and I have just become one.
*The White Pathway lies in front of me: it is not
    crossed by the Blue.*
*The white hair from the crown of my head is to
    alight upon the White Chair,*
which will be elevating me unto the sky.
*Long Man, You who took Your origin from the
    water-seep,*

You have just come to put the White Walkingstick into my hand.

COMMENTARY by Jack Frederick Kilpatrick and Anna Gritts Kilpatrick (who collected, edited, and translated these texts)

'[T]he great body of medico-religious writings of the Cherokees is their true literature, and . . . one of the most profound and sublime productions of the creative spirit of man . . . The 'Going to the Water' . . . are the most impressive of all of the ceremonies of the Cherokee and are performed only on important occasions, such as the birth of a child, the death of a relative or a very close friend, to obtain long life . . . Most of the 'Going to the Water' rites are enacted at dawn while facing the sacred direction East at the brink of a flowing stream.'[39]

'[T]he water spirit bestows upon the communicant various symbols of a 'white' (and therefore serene and revered) old age – a cloth, a chair, a walking stick, and hair. . . . An individual, a pair of mates, or a family group begins the recitation of a longevity prayer upon leaving home, and terminates it upon reaching the brink of running

water. (Most Cherokee homes are built within a short distance of a creek or a spring.) There follows a ceremonial laving of the hands and face, or else immersion.'[40]

4

Water Becomes Difference

I

At regular intervals, viral TikTok videos emerge showing a line that separates the Atlantic from the Pacific waters, one side frothy dark blue, the other a gentle green grey. It seems we are thirsty for such spectaculars of separability. They satisfy something primordial, individuality within collectivity, togetherness in difference, a counter-intuitive miracle of sorts.

As usual, TikTok does not quite hold the whole truth, but it does give access to a fleeting velleity. While the videos in question are not doctored, their waters are not of oceans but of rivers and glaciers that feed the ocean and create the apparent difference.[1] Does this mean that ocean waters always mix? Not necessarily. Even when they do and become eventually indistinguishable, mixing doesn't happen immediately but depends on differences in temperature, purity or salinity, and turbulence.[2] But, more often than not, rather than mixing, oceans simply 'exchange waters': waters from different oceans can be found sliding next to one another, their differences retained (although not remotely as TikTokable).

These large slices of oceanic depths are called 'clines', a word etymologically derived from the ancient Greek noun *klinē* (κλίνη 'couch'; 'bier') and verb *klinein* (κλίνειν 'to recline'). Masses of water retain their individual characteristics while gliding next to other masses of water. The word 'cline' shares its etymon with the Latin *clinamen* – a noun coined by Lucretius to translate the original Epicurean term *parenklisis* (παρέγκλισις), which famously designated the swerving or inclination of atoms. In Epicurus' ontology, this angle of inclination brought about further movement and contingent consequences. Clinamen is the first step in the butterfly effect of planetary changes.

Deleuze employs clinamen as 'the reciprocal determination'[3] of molecules to move in relation to one another, to slide next to one another, to mix and synthesise. In the context of water, clinamen would be the desire of bodies of water both to flow into one ('determination') and to retain their difference ('reciprocal'). 'Aquatic clinamen' is a propensity of molecular material towards mixing, that is, towards becoming one, and it is premised on the material need to remain different: waters need to remain different in order to swap; yet what is swapped is fundamentally the same ontological matter. Clinamen is aquatic agency: desire to be one, desire to be other, and a perpetual, unquenchable desire *not* to choose between states, always to slide from one state to the other in this tightly circumscribed freedom.

Clinamen is the aqueous space of the desire to become one while remaining separate. This is the ultimate love story.

2

'Water becomes difference', writes Neimanis.[4] Water gestates other bodies of water, different yet contiguous. But, even before that, water embodies its agency in clines, humans, geological strata: in short, through its membrane containment, its momentary rupture from the 'other' water, its solidification or gasification. Like any love story, this is a tale of resisting time, however temporary, inefficient, or futile this might be. In separation there is a passage of desire into rupturing, into withdrawing, into being elsewhere, finally otherwise.

But this is not a unidirectional desire. It is a spread out, horizontal desire that covers the globe and its bodies. It's a polyamorous, mycelian desire, in which bodies glide along multiple other bodies, inclining towards becoming other yet retaining their individuality. This is a double conative desire, to be both separate and one. Water's conatus is that of clinamen, but the desire to mix is always predicated on the ontology of difference. And, vice versa, the desire to rupture away and to assert one's one body in difference never cancels the ontological continuum of water.

Barad's agential separability encapsulates the continuum, where difference resists homogenisation, whatever the pressure.[5] Separability itself can be a cherished source of identity: in the context of saltwater tribes in Australia (themselves less discussed moieties that, unlike the majority of Aboriginal tribes, are water- rather than land-based) anthropologist Nonie Sharp writes: 'the Yolŋu are keen observers of their world: they see salt waters and fresh waters swirling at the river mouths, spreading forth as two separate streams that never fully merge into one another, yet travel together'.[6] The water moieties know what to observe, what to cherish, what to distinguish, and how to draw identity from such differences.

Yet one overarching theme emerges at all times in hydrotheory: the other side of the rupture is not an outside, but part of the continuum with the ruptured body. As *quilombola* thinker Antônio Bispo dos Santos puts it, 'a river does not stop being a river because it confluences with another river; on the contrary, it becomes itself and other rivers, it becomes stronger'.[7] Confluence is predicated on separability – and vice versa.

The previous chapter was dedicated to passages or movements that perpetuate the continuum. In this chapter I would like to focus on passages that, while part of the continuum, make a difference by placing distance between bodies of water and by allowing for other waters to emerge. With this, we have the fulness of hydrojustice: continuum and difference; not just oneness but proliferation, promiscuity, profligacy, polyamory; not just return but departure, line of flight, withdrawal. How is it possible to balance these two seemingly opposing forces? Or, better, to preserve their ontological balancing without imagining facile homeostatic heavens? How to accept difference without threat? How to accept conflict without demonising it? How to accept that post-crisis means a new hydroreality of immeasurable, so far unknowable consequences? How to adapt to something that we, as humans, have been systematically ignoring, in arrogant defiance?

So, while keeping in mind the continuum, in what follows I focus on this rather arbitrary epistemological distinction: the 'other' water, both *as* the ruptured water and *as* the new body of water that emerges after the rupture.

3

Over the past few decades, a system has been planned that would save Venice from the ever-rising, ever more frequent flooding. Part of it is a form of floodgates, finally completed in 2020 amid resistance from the local and international community – a resistance caused by their excessive costs and associated corruption scandals, their inability to future-proof against climate change water rise (since the early 1900s, the mean sea level in Venice increased about 35 cm),[8] and their impact on the lagoon and its biotic processes. The waters are indeed stopped from rushing into Venice, but the environmental impact on the lagoon is already considerable.[9] For context, the Venice lagoon covers an area of 550 km², 67 per cent of which is covered by water, 25 per cent by saltmarshes, and 8 per cent by the islands. Venice itself covers a mere 8 km² or 1.4 per cent of the total area.

The dam is part of a wider project called MoSE, an acronym for *modulo sperimentale elettromeccanico* (experimental electromechanical module). This name is evidently related to the profoundly Christian history of the Serenissima: it evokes Moses's parting of the waters – the moment when he raised his hand to allow two walls of water to go up and form a path in the middle for his people to escape the Egyptians.

True to their name, the MoSE floodgates separate the waters: through a hydraulic system, they rise every time the tide is predicted to be damaging for Venice. It is not a regular dam, but operates like one when the floodgates are raised. In other words, there is a moment when the waters are separated: waters coming into the lagoon from the open sea are either stopped (if too high) or allowed to continue (if regular).

The separation of waters is the moment when rupture emerges.

Any rupture in the aquatic continuum is part of a series of ruptures – indeed, a continuum of ruptures. The continuum emerges through the circularity of ruptures, heads of Hydra in their fall and regeneration, a blooming of ruptures, a monstrous continuum: the emollient that might save us.

4

With every raising of the MoSE floodgates, freedom of choice emerges.

With every raising of the MoSE floodgates, the illusion of choice emerges.

In Venice larger decisions are now at stake: in view of the continually rising waters, the MoSE will soon be inadequate. Existing natural solutions, such as the salt marshes that have traditionally offered protection, have been affected by various interventions.[10] A radical solution is to shut off the lagoon to saline water completely and make it instead a closed lake-like lagoon. Venice the city will be saved, but the old lagoon will die and a new, very different one will eventually emerge, with its associated risks for all bodies involved. As environmental scientists Davide Tagliapietra and Georg Umgiesser put it, we can save either Venice or the lagoon. Not both.[11]

Whether the lagoon is sealed off to save Venice or Venice is allowed to sink in order to save the lagoon, a new kind of body of water will be generated. Water becoming difference: there is melancholy whatever the decision, there is violence in the act of deciding, there is force in the urgency of time, but there is also a necessity to maintain boundaries between waters.

Rupture is separation. It is withdrawal from the ubiquitous continuum, even if this withdrawal is temporary. It is the illusion of the other side, indeed of an outside. And it is also the illusion of choice, freedom, decision.

Often the only choice truly available hides behind the illusion. In the ethics of shared flow, this is the responsibility to withdraw, to leave it alone, as Elena Glasberg writes: 'I heard Antarctica's icy shores endlessly repeat a simple message: "go away".'[12]

5

Parts of Fiji's reefs are circumscribed by barnacled pillars embedded in the reef floor. The interruption of the flatness is discrete, but its signalling is clear: this is a no-fishing area. 'Tabu', the traditional characterisation of off limits areas, used to be marked with sticks on the reef and a coconut leaf tied on them. This practice denoted the temporary separation of the waters for 100 days after a chief's death – a space of grief and regeneration. The practice is currently used as a fishing management tool, and it has an impressive record for reef regeneration.[13]

Taking the decision to separate the waters, indeed to revive an old tradition that had fallen into desuetude, is a recognisable instance of distributive justice, boosted by the juridical desire for demarcation and distribution – *nomos*. But these are not lines of positivist or neoliberal marine management in the sense found in the usual hegemonic territorial discourses, appropriated by legal 'stakeholders'.[14] Tabu does not work against, but along 'the unwritten and un-inscribable being of the sea'.[15] Tabu does not denote sovereignty markings but a togetherness based on separation, a propinquity based on distance: these markings are, properly speaking, the commons. Goodrich writes: '*nomos* written on water . . . common law . . . The law of amity is the law of a strange proximity, a law of togetherness, of the sharing of being.'[16]

At the core of the commons lies a space of aqueous aporia: what is shared is keeping off limits. Nothing is distributed here. Hydrojustice emerges in this negative, 'no-resource' space within the aquatic continuum, this 'angelological space, a purely imagistic and vanishing domain'.[17] This is not John Selden's *mare clausum* (closed sea), which we wrap around us in lines of sovereign demarcation in order to feel safe. What keeps this space negative is not presence but absence, not law but justice.

Withdrawing along the imaginary lines of separation does not, of course, interrupt the aquatic continuum. If anything, it serves it by sustaining it. As the locals say, the reefs have never looked better. The future is nestled with care in the folds of the rupture: no longer connected to anthropic loss, the tabu manages to embrace the grief for a vaster ecological loss and to do something about it by not doing anything. This is a quiet, confident *désoeuvrement* (undoing) that positions a body of water at the centre of the continuum and demarcates it as difference.

6

For part of the year the Cambodian village of Kampong Phluk remains dry, while for the other part it becomes aquatic, half-submerged, slower, wetter. For geographers Philip Steinberg and Kimberley Peters, the fluctuation between the two states forces us to rethink relations of verticality and their connection to the standard human way of existing.[18]

To live an amphibian life is an exercise in horizontality: whether it is the amphibian animal that crawls and floats or the waters that slide and ebb, the confluence between one and the other body of water (say, the village on the one hand and the ocean on the other) spreads across the surface of the earth, creating its own temporality of ruptures.

I remember watching, at Whitechapel Gallery in London, 'That Which Is to Come Is Just a Promise', a 2019 short film by the Italian art collective Flatform in which the dry and the wet were playfully placed in a dreamy succession: it was almost a superimposition of seasons on Funafuti Atoll, so that even dryness acquired a fluidity of anticipation and nostalgia for the wet. The artists followed the village dwellers walking on dirt roads in what seemed like a somnolent afternoon, lulled by the anticipation of the next scene, in which the exact same path became indistinguishable from the wetness around it.

On that flat horizontality, the diagonal is freed as a new body of water.

This slow pace of the itinerant human unshackles the body from the directionality of the carved road and gently ushers it into a diagonal that crosses fields and gardens, saturated in the wet regression of Hydrogeos.

7

Water molecules tremble with clinamen.

From its surface tension to its gaseous propensity to take up all available space, water is animated by an agency beyond volition. And humans follow that agency, listening to our bodies as they create aquatic narratives like sketches on the surface of the sea: frothy lines that connect spaces of aporia.

Perhaps one of the best depictions of this aquatic clinamen is John Cheeve's 1964 short story 'The Swimmer', subsequently made into a film in 1968. The film was directed by Eleanor and Frank Perry and featured Burt Lancaster in the role (if you would allow me) of the clinamen. The swimmer creates a narrative line of connection among the separated waters of the bourgeois American dream, their big houses and their even bigger private pools. He decides to swim on that line: 'In his mind he saw, with a cartographer's eye, a string of swimming pools, a quasi-subterranean stream that curved across the county.'[19]

Constantly diving and emerging, the swimmer explores his own continuum with the water (Lancaster's blue eyes are all the time emphasised in relation to the pool waters). He starts by floating in Dostoyevskian innocence, traversing private properties, chic pool parties, inane conversations, and even time itself, as he moves diagonally back and forth between various ages, lovers, and connections in his life: 'the day was lovely, and that he lived in a world so generously supplied with water seemed like a clemency, a beneficence'. Everything around him ushers him forth, making him part of the watery transformation, inviting him into the folds of a sparkling river: 'the water refracted the sound of voices and laughter and seemed to suspend it in midair'. Yet he fiercely remains separate from his surroundings. He is often the only one scantily dressed in his swimming trunks, and he dreams of escaping that settled society of cocktail drinkers.

But the story is saturated with hubris right from the start, and the swimmer is soon drowning in his own machismo, poisoned by the chlorinated boxes of advanced capitalism.[20] What begins as the dream of a misguided continuum ends up being the realisation of an inevitable rupture. In the film, he finally arrives home, only to be greeted by torrential rain: another water, diffused and aerated, very different from the comfortable containment of the pools, a water that exposes the swimmer's inability to map, name, and control. We understand now that his aquatic narrative was simply a desperate attempt to defy and defeat the ultimate rupture for human consciousness: death. His swimming across ruptures was his way of living forever, surfing on his youthful looks and making his home in a simple reenactment of being alive.

Rupture means that we must respect the limits. We must not succumb to the illusionary promise of the continuum, that desire for an open space full of freedom and choice. For the continuum carries on independently of our volition, and we are invariably left behind, desperately thinking of quick fixes.

8

For many hydrotheorists, for example Amimoto Ingersoll and her seascape epistemology,[21] swimming and diving are ways of embracing the continuum of the individual bodies with the vast body of water. In hydroqueer theory, 'to just keep swimming is to embrace aqueous eroticisms of human, queer, and more-than-human kinds'.[22]

Perhaps counterintuitively, I would suggest that, in swimming, water becomes difference. When swimming, the body embraces not just the continuum but also the desire to remain separate. The former is the conative desire to be fully permeated by water, a body like a sieve, which does not impose but fully participates. The other side of the conative desire is to retain one's life, one's positionality and one's awareness of positionality within the vastness. Swimming is both these sides.

Swimming embodies the clinamen.

Using the way a swimmer's body connects to the sea as an example, Deleuze explores the forms of knowledge in Spinoza. Thus the first degree refers to someone who cannot swim and whose experience of water is nervous, angular, violent. The second degree of knowledge is represented by a reasonably able swimmer, who follows the water movement, in continuous adjustment of their own position. Finally, the third degree is an almost under-the-skin understanding of the modalities of body and water, so perfect that the swimmer comes close to becoming one with the aquatic continuum.[23]

While understandably one would aspire towards the third form of knowledge, I find Deleuze's second degree more conducive to human responsibility towards the planet, and closer to the practice of hydrojustice. The second degree, with its constant readjustment, its doubts and uncertainties, its hesitant positioning and somewhat modest appreciation of one's abilities, is aligned to an attempt at fitting in rather than mastering. Paddling rather than immersion. Sliding along rather than demarcating. The Swimmer discovers this at the end, when, defeated and weathered, resigns himself to dwelling on the rupture.

9

With every rupture, a new body of water emerges and joins the continuum.

A contemporary Jewish interpretation of the separation of waters in Genesis has come to us via Leo Strauss, who claims that separation, distinction, and categorisation are Genesis' standard tricks. For Strauss, the main distinction is the one between otherness and motion. Motion is pivotal in his view: 'it means not merely for a thing to be separated from other things but to be able to separate itself from its place'.[24] To move from one's given place is often a result of displacement, violence, rejection. In some cases a body has no choice but to move.

But, even in such cases, there is always the possibility that a new body of water would emerge. Tuvalu, one of the Pacific Islands states threatened by rising seawaters, imagines a future without land. Already seawater seeps through the soil, endangering crops and drinking water resources. What is a state without land? What is a state made of closing waves?

The constitution has been amended so that Tuvalu remains a state in perpetuity in the future, notwithstanding the impact of climate change or other factors that may cause loss of physical territory. For the past few years, Tuvalu has been steadily accumulating its traditions, customs, language, and a light detection and ranging (LiDAR) scan of its 124 islands in a living cultural archive curated by its citizens, in order to transition to the cloud.[25] This is a different water, a virtual water (virtual also in the Deleuzian sense of being not actual but still real) immaterial yet grounded in data warehouses and bitcoin community mechanisms, floating about like an arc simulation that avidly consumes non-renewables.

Ruptures are not always welcome. They shake us out of a comfortable inertia, in which things keep on rolling and no consideration is given to detrimental consequences. Our usual verticality means that 'business as usual' puts at a disadvantage the weaker bodies, the low-lying poorer nations, the urban poor in cities threatened by floods and landslides, the enduring vertical heritage of colonialism and the marching of capitalism.

I hesitate to embark on a list of vertical ruptures. The simple mention of some of them would take up the whole book. Dams, rivers, water sources are becoming spaces of extraction and, in the process, disrupt the connection between water 'and the people who live, work, and remember on its banks and amongst its flows', rendering both humans and multispecies life 'surplus, a hindrance to the accumulation of profit and thus susceptible to violence', as hydrotheorist and artist Ifor Duncan writes.[26] This is necrohydrology: the instrumental rupture 'between "natural" and "unnatural" waters', a concept in which the latter (toxic rain, lowering reservoirs, dewatering, ground contamination, etc.) are turned against the horizontality of waters. These are ruptures co-opted and corrupted, organised in the name of a voracious verticality, made to pose as progress, freedom of choice, economic and sovereign rationality.

But allow me to mention a strikingly abhorrent redeployment of verticality that emerged recently, in the usual form of technological advancement. The first commercial octopus farm is being built in Spain and feeds global hunger for the octopus (350,000 tonnes annually).[27] Images of Nueva Pescanova, the company's research and development headquarters in Galicia, offer a taste of what this venture is about: on the first floor, there are state-of-the-art meeting rooms and offices where feats of what is recognised beyond doubt as human intelligence take place. Right underneath, on the ground floor and in the basement, octopuses – modified so as to have their tendency for propulsion curtailed, which limits their territoriality and allows them to cohabit with other octopuses at close quarters – are left lying in shallow waters in multiple identical tanks, a dystopian vision of a lesser people.

The octopus, as is well known, embodies a multiplicity of intelligence forms, where all limbs have their own separate brain and retain autonomy from the rest of the body. Yet the argument here is not to refrain from eating intelligent species; this would be a fatuous position, which attempts to cover up many other critical considerations. In a symbolic sense, here we have the continuum, with its ruptures linked by clinamen: a farm filled with Hydras, which wait to be served with potatoes.

In an anticipated pro-farming argument, the company has publicly questioned the perceived intelligence of octopuses.[28] And that should settle the argument.

10

Passages are often also aesthetic: Tuvalu's foreign minister, Simon Kofe, famously delivered his 2022 COP26 address standing in seawater up to his thighs. The video starts with the image of a politician in a suit who delivers a speech against the usual background of flags, and it progressively zooms out to take in the reality of the water.

We learn to live in a new ontopolitical reality by engaging with emerging bodies of water. In a bittersweet piece about her native Oceanside in California, art historian Amber Hickey shares how the continuous ruptures introduced by war testing forced her to love a different kind of home: 'the strange affection I have for those reverberations remains, uncomfortably, with me, like the closeness I feel with the contaminated ocean – my toxic, watery kin'.[29] This affection is not resignation but a clinamen that slides with the new reality, without accepting it as good or finite: 'though I am hopeful that the ocean will someday be liberated from its toxicity, the love I have for it is unconditional'.

Rupture means learning to recognise new continua and new ways of adapting to the continuum.

11

Let us dive in. Let us open a deep horizontality, which resists the phallic verticality of fracking, drilling, extracting. Let us slide between the clines without recourse to resource.

When pregnant Africans were thrown overboard the slave ships, their foetuses started swimming in a much larger womb, gently carried by the ocean. In Kodwo Eshun's words, Drexciyans, the mysterious 'aqua people' who produced Detroit techno in the late 1990s, started sliding underwater, in anaerobic respiration: 'Could it be possible for humans to breathe underwater? A foetus in its mother's womb is certainly alive in an aquatic environment. Is it possible that they could have given birth at sea to babies that never needed air?'[30]

Breathing underwater is not some sort of neo-colonialist fantasy about the apophatic depths of the seas. It is a moment of withdrawal from what we consider humanity, a gasp of nostalgia for our gill-covered past, a lapping regression towards a hushed life, an Afrofuturist dare. Think of the Bajau people in the Malay Archipelago who spend 60 per cent of their working day underwater for as long as five minutes at a time.[31] Or think of the Kanaka surfer, who 'has learned that she must remember her human "dive reflex", an automatic reduction in heart rate and oxygen consumption'.[32] This is a trained human, but also a human who remembers her aquatic origin, nestling in that open space of not imposing, not taking, not exploiting – just floating along. As Neimanis writes, 'between inspiration and expiration, there is always a small gap – a pause really, where we are breathing neither in, nor out. We simply hover.'[33]

This aspiration for the depths is not a verticality but a gentle horizontality: a slicing of the depths in thick clines of belonging. In the cities of the flooded future, upside-down climbers create surfaces of anaerobic existence between the clines of waters from past eras. These surfaces are cutting across the verticality of our high-rise buildings, our communication antennas, our fracking shafts, our launch routes to space exploration. And we, neither human nor water, we, the tentative hydrohumans, glide on these surfaces, perhaps with technological mediation, or perhaps just on our newly rediscovered gills, exploring the horizontality of the deep.

12

In the Danish pavilion of the 2021 Venice Art Biennale, two oversized and unnervingly lifelike centaurs lie dying. A female centaur who has just given birth lies dead or unconscious on the floor, the new-born still in its amniotic sac. In the room next to it, the male centaur is hanging from the ceiling, his powerful neck reduced to a bunch of non-pulsing sinews, his six limbs hanging lifeless over the heads of visitors. He could have been the father who killed himself, unable to bear the birth of a child in this world: he had the freedom to decide his end, when the total end has already been decided for him. In Uffe Isolotto's exhibition *We Walked the Earth* we witness the intimate death spasm of the last human hybrids.

The accompanying brochure is a short story by Jacob Lillemose that begins with these words: 'There is water everywhere. Everywhere we have ever been and where we are now. Water is our life. We're made to live *in* water, and we're made *of* water.' It soon becomes obvious that we are talking about something more adventurous than another hydrotheoretical approach: 'Not the same water that surrounds our body, although it could easily be mistaken for it. The water that is our body is the new water. A water filled with miniscule units that allow us to transform our bodies into anything at all.' And so it starts, the journey of lapping Ovidian transformation of this unidentified 'we' with 'no fixed form or dimensions'. We join this journey of continuous encounters with other bodies, a vertiginous clinamen of different waters.

We are given a small, tentative hope: not a hope that humanity will continue the way it is, but a hope that humans might be discovered by other bodies, the shifting water molecules, explorative, playful, alien yet part of us. Might this be the new hydrohuman? Humanity's sequence? A diffused consciousness that shapeshifts and bounces in our bodily crevices and valleys, where our existence used to surface?

13

Sometimes, when trying to fall asleep, I shut my eyes and conjure up a holiday room that my family and I stayed in when I was little. It was a brief stay, a couple of days perhaps, part of a road trip we took in northern Greece.

The accommodation was sparse, the beds uncomfortable, the walls weathered. Yet the focus of the room (and of my somnolence) was the window.

The window opened directly onto a lake.

It did not open onto the lake shore, or even onto a little patch of land that the waves would lick, but right onto the lake. Opening the window meant stretching over the surface of the lake. The water would reach a few centimetres below the window, caressing the sill from underneath. In different weather the waves would go much higher, if the marks on the wall were anything to go by. But during the two days of our visit, drenched as we were in the Greek summer heat, the water was a gentle sheet of wavelets and the window was kept constantly open, so that the light breeze would touch our bodies as we tried to sleep.

That window has always enticed me, whether in the reality of the actual experience or in my reminiscing mind. Still in my pyjamas, I climb out of the window and float out as gently as I can, quietly and unobtrusively, full of timid care for the life around me, the life I am leaving behind, and the life that is floating, swimming, or crawling just outside that window.

I slowly lower myself in the warm water, an amnion of the continuum.

I keep close to the wall. The water is shallow and inviting, reaching up to my thighs. I walk a little further out, deep enough to sit slowly on the bed of the lake. I invite the liquid in my body through my pores. I let my liquid ooze out from me, breath and sweat and humidity, a material and metaphorical moment where the human fluvial is gliding into the planetary. I look around. There is a gurgle of activity: seaweed, fish, pebbles reflecting light and then disappearing, dunes moving along the lakebed that mirrors the waves above.

The more I let go, the more the water forgets me. When I finally exhale all the air inside me, when I see the other water traversing my skin, when I am me but diffused, sliced, sluiced, permeable, then everything expands like a wave of time, gigantically slow.

The waters forget me somewhere among their folds. They let me observe the pause. I am inside the great outside, diluted into foamy oblivion.[34]

14

Rupture is the ethical testing ground of hydrojustice. Respecting limits and difference (since radical otherness is never possible in Hydrogeos) requires a continuous, hesitant, palindromic negotiation on how best to slide next to one another, how to partition one's water body, how to share it, and even how to allow it to diffuse.

If locally embodied, law can help. But this is a horizontal law, law as water, law of bodies in and of water. Indigenous tribes in Kenya use law to work through irrigation: 'Water distribution is decided through meetings . . . often very informal and impromptu affairs. Allocation is constantly being negotiated.'[35] Codifiable, 'formal' rules and 'working', contextualised, flexible rules coexist side by side with 'rules' against rules ('water is shared, sold, and stolen'), all contributing to a continuous rupture that brings about even the inclusion of traditionally less included bodies (e.g. the practice of stealing water paradoxically permits near equal access to water for women who are traditionally excluded from it. In Canada, the visionary Nibi ('Water') Declaration of Treaty #3 – on the entanglement between the Anishinaabe citizens and Nibi on their territory – codifies such rules (spiritual, natural, customary, and human law) under one ethical umbrella: they are 'based on relationships as opposed to rights and obligations' and are ruled by 'generalized reciprocity, where beings have a responsibility to one another'.[36]

While the continuum focuses on common elementality, rupture focuses on the boundaries between singular elementalities. This is hydrojustice: negotiation of positioning, acceptance of dissolution and conflict, preparation for new emergences. Goodrich suitably invents: '*Aequitas*, to coin a phrase, is the law of the aquatic, or, to attempt a maxim of my own, *in mare semper est aequitas* – equity is the essence of the sea because like equity, the sea expands and contracts, insufflates and exhales, opens and closes according to a temporality, a lunacy, all its own.'[37] And folded in between those exhalations are bodies that inhabit ruptures.

Ruptures often appear as decisions about options, whether human or planetary. But, if placed on the horizontality of planetary aquatic interest, the real options become clear. These are the ethics of the *shared flow*, as I show below: not a question of who has the power to decide according to their interest, but rather a dissolution of the usual verticality of decision-making in favour of horizontality, an ethics of flow that emerges from how the bodies array themselves and how they incline towards one another. There is no 'human free will' in all this. It is all inscribed in the folds of hydrojustice.

Ruptures (in the form of decisions) give rise to emergent bodies of water. We are all part of this emergence: a new post-crisis horizontality, deeply unpredictable and irreversibly destabilising, is upon us. Bodies, emergencies, future: all form part of this very horizontality.

Wavewriting IV

Repeat

On an island surrounded by the Southern Ocean, an arduous ascending trail carves a pathway between a river and a mountain range. This trail, which I will call the 'Track', is a border zone between urban developments and the wilderness the island is known for. As the human population increases, the 'Track' is becoming more susceptible to damage, becoming gradually wider, with vegetation being pushed back and the dense basalt rock face becoming exposed . . .

I have carried a large heavyweight roll of French imported paper, 18 metres long and over a metre wide . . . I soak the roll of paper in the waterhole, which is deeper than I thought. The boots, socks and tights come off as I enter the freezing water to gently unravel the paper down the creek bed ensuring the water soaks into every fibre of the paper. With difficulty, as my feet, blue with cold, are stabbed by the rocks and branches in the creek bed, I drag the paper up on to a section of the 'Track'. The paper settles along the indentations and curvature of the 'Track' wending its way around a bend and beyond sight . . . The soaked fibrous surface reveals the contours of what lies beneath, like the membrane of skin over our bodies, the hard, bony skeleton of the earth presses and stretches the surface. This membrane inhales the touch of everything it comes into contact with, retaining traces of a memory of an encounter across space, time, matter: a 'contract.'

This large roll of paper is a witness to the exchanges that occur on the 'Track', shifting the prevalence of law's discourse where a contract is considered an 'arms-length' transaction between two parties, to a haptic natureculture continuum where the laws of nature are acknowledged and entwined in humanity's legal theories.

I spend over a year revisiting the 'Track' each week with the roll of paper.[38]

Jan Hogan

5

Wavewriting

I

Italo Calvino's *Mr Palomar* begins with the narrator 'reading a wave'. His aim is to look at a single wave and read its textuality, its wet paragraphs and moist references, understand the way it unfolds on the page of the world. But he soon discovers that 'isolating one wave is not easy, separating it from the wave immediately following ... or from the preceding wave'.[1]

The word for world is wave, to paraphrase Ursula Le Guin. But, more than that, the word *of* world is wave. Mr Palomar tries to take in a single wave *as* the world; not a representation, a symbol, or a signifier *of* the world, not even a phenomenon *in* the world. He understands that everything is here, on the surface. But if the wave is the world, how is it that every wave is at the same time different *and* every other wave, preceding and following? How is it that every wave diffracts into a myriad of selves?[2] That every wave is written across time in the same planetary incantation?[3]

Mr Palomar tries to perceive the wave 'beyond sensory and mental habits'. He posits himself as the ultimate anti-phenomenologist: wave is world. But how can a human ride the world while remaining humble, aware of being only a part of it all and not the central actor? There is only one position to adopt: slowly slide into the world, next to the wave, like a Deleuzian swimmer, diagonally cutting the wave,[4] aware of the difference and the continuum with the wave, emulating without controlling, hesitantly but persistently: 'water has a syntax I am still learning'.[5]

And repeat. And repeat. As in philosopher Michel Serres's chapter 'La belle noiseuse' ('The Beautiful Troublemaker'):[6] the recurring ruckus of waves, the rhythm that sounds the world. But also with finitude: we need to let the wave boom itself out, reach its peak, become the last wave.

We need to believe that this will be the last ever wave, the one that will flood and change everything. But we should also imagine what happens after the wave is gone, or at least know that the wave will be gone and that, although it might well be the last ever wave, there is always one after that.

We must *ride* both crest and trough.

2

We must *write* both crest and trough.

Reading the world, riding the wave, writing hydrojustice: as a writing method, hydrojustice relies on feeling the text of the water writing itself into a text that defies abusive structures, exploitative dams, exclusionary culverts.

Let us call this 'wavewriting': an ondoyant writing methodology, 'the language of waveshape'.[7]

Wavewriting has its own sound. It's the Vanuatu women, waist-deep in the ocean, slashing and creating water music: *vus lamlam* or rupturing the water, an emulation of the wave, a writing over and along the wave; a rough melody, a gurgle, a circularity, a palindromic incantation;[8] or Richard Strauss' *Der Rosenkavalier* – possibly one of the dullest operas in the global repertoire, yet with two or three devastatingly beautiful passages. The finale with three sopranos is wavewritten: sound wavelets from multiple directions, confluence and conflict, a constantly postponed gratification, particle explosions of desire at every note, a rupture of expectations; no real finale. The final note sprays away, a non-concluding diagonal.

This book has been a modest exercise in wavewriting: small waves, not showy; inviting yet corrosive. The waves remain part of a continuum, while each one, separately, forms a rupture. This is a precariously contained river text, with puddling *ciénagas* (swamps) that resist the monolinearity of mapping:[9] it has short sections that follow the reader's sharp breaths, wavelets of affective involvement in which the reader is invited to float, gingerly feeling their way amid the wavewriting.

Wavewriting accommodates the three meanings of the word *nalu* in the Hawai'ian Kanaka language: 'wave'; 'to ponder' and 'to speculate'; and 'amnion, amniotic fluid'.[10] This is wavewriting both as a tending of the future and as a return.

Wavewriting involves multiple definitions, multiple angles, multiple disciplines; a diffractive gestation of new emergences; focus on one wave and one world, while knowing that there is no such thing as one wave, because there is no one world; focus on the last wave, knowing that there will always be more waves after the last. Write fast, write also the pauses.

3

Water puddles the space between the paragraphs, crowns the apostrophes, sprays up the footnotes. Water writes the words, water reads them, water writes the world. The poet Rita Wong writes: 'a watery lexicon and syntax, a hydrological approach could cultivate our capacity to scale down to the level of molecules and up to the level of oceans'.[11]

This text is water. It has always been water: agency is neither awarded nor discovered. Agency is the conative thrust behind every word of every flesh of every text of every sea. Agency is the continuum of water. Agency is the rupture of water in gliding clines. Agency is what acts behind every action.

But water is also flesh.

Referring to Merleau-Ponty, Pugliese writes: 'water is always already a body enfleshed …

only ever intelligible through the different bodies of water – drops, mists, rivers, oceans'.[12] The vocabulary of hydrojustice, the vocabulary of the world's aquatic flesh as it is written on the earth's surface, needs to be fleshed forth.

Hydrojustice as method opens up a linguistic surface on which bodies of water move. It brings together living language and pulsing flesh, placing in between them only flow.

Hydrojustice is a *fleshy* or *material metaphor*: a concept that slides between the linguistic and the material and transfers meaning across to both.[13] Quoting the Stoic Chrysippus, Deleuze writes: 'If you say something, it passes through your lips: so, if you say "chariot", a chariot passes through your lips.'[14] Fleshy metaphors perform a sliding between folds of the same surface that are often thought of as opposing – between language and materiality, between my body of water and the bodies of other humans or nonhumans, or between different disciplines, practices, and ways of knowing and making: 'water is the ultimate medium for the conversations that continually create the world'.[15]

As a fleshy metaphor, hydrojustice links up continuum and rupture, making the connection between language and water tangible. Hydrojustice means that, when waters rise, languages become extinct.[16] Tuvaluan, Kiribati, and Marshallese, the languages native to the low-lying atolls of the Pacific, are already considered endangered. Amimoto Ingersoll writes: 'the ocean is involved in the writing and reading process, affecting how we create and shape both ourselves and our nations'.[17] Hydrojustice means that, in order to speak with water, one needs to make up a new vocabulary, a new language, beyond the representational and deep into the metaphorical. Yes, there is 'continuity between the speech of water and the speech of [hu]man',[18] as Gaston Bachelard writes. But water speech is an openness to the fleshy metaphorical, a material and fleshy speech that communicates primarily with movement.

4

As a method of writing, therefore, hydrojustice asks for pausing, observing the flow, allowing the text to write itself, riding the text, feeling the text surging from one's hands, marvelling at the text's palindrome, at the way it moves back and forth and around concepts and movements, at the way it never quite gives you what you thought you wanted when you started reading it, but moves your body so as to allow your flesh to become one with it.

As a method of being, hydrojustice asks for moving, sliding, hesitating, thinking, not thinking, claiming, accepting, dying, diffusing, becoming. It is an ontological state, a time of post-crisis emergency, a recovered horizontality, an animated surface. Above all, hydrojustice is an embodiment, a being in body – whether one's own narrowly identifiable body or the vast aquatic continuum that extends beyond the planet.

As a method of political action, hydrojustice asks us to be water, to move diagonally and recapture the horizontality, to strategise our movement but also to flow in any way and on any path possible while in clinamen, riding both distance and propinquity, both continuum and rupture. Hydrojustice offers the space to negotiate by confluence or separation, but this is not free choice (although it offers spaces of choice), nor is it a prescribed political horizon. Hydrojustice cannot be instrumentalised in terms of its meaning or its goals. It is a question of constant negotiation, palindromic decision-making, perpetual refusal to settle, encompassing much grander time and space cycles than traditional anthropocentric or even ecocentric justice.

As a method of being with, hydrojustice asks for loving even more than for caring: loving gently, carefully, hesitantly, openly; loving the waters within and the waters without; loving in 'relationality, responsibility and reciprocity', the way the Yukon First Nation respects, fears, loves water;[19] loving by turning away from the face, because a body of water has no face; loving away from the adversarial, sliding wherever the body slides in the water, following the direction that the wave – and the body as wave – gives itself; loving the passage and the stoppage; loving the water monster and all her heads, loving the rupture and the constant flow of extending infinities. Become a sieve, see yourself refracted. Hydrojustice is a polyamorous project in and with the agency of water, a skin erotics that becomes planet.

Above all, as a method of becoming, it means that one always embodies hydrojustice. Hydrojustice is a conative thrust.

5

What determines the direction of this thrust?

There's a saying, shared by the languages of the eastern Mediterranean, which sets out an ethical scheme as watery as the geography of the cultures themselves, as porous as the ethnic and linguistic crossflow of the region: 'do the good deed and throw it in the sea'. This simple idiom posits openness as aquatic ethics: by casting it in the water, one removes the good deed from the economy of exchange.

One casts the good deed along the shore, like a paper boat on a quiet evening: a secret, a confession, a fragile moment of strength shared with our soft watery inside. For there is a circularity in the deed of casting, a return of the deed to its womb, an understanding of what is needed and what is demanded. And yet we know that this inside is seamlessly linked to a vast outside: a cosmic clinamen that reveals an ethical position. In modern Greek, this saying uses the word *gialos* ('shore'), which is reminiscent of the word *giali*, 'glass' – looking glass, the reflective surface that returns the self. It means '[t]rusting in someone that is bigger than ourselves', writes

Ibrahim Nehme, commenting on the Lebanese version of the same saying – trusting our deed in 'a reflection of the vastness within us, of our inherent good nature'.[20] The deed is carried by waves, found by mermaids and castaways, and perhaps, who knows, returned to the one who casts it in some sort of aquatic form: *per grazia ricevuta*, 'for the grace received' – the formula we encounter on votive images of ships saved from wild seas.

This is the ethics of hydrojustice: a *shared flow* of ethical positioning; a clinamen of the reciprocal desire to slide along one another. 'Water makes ethics possible',[21] as Mielle Chandler and Astrida Neimanis write, but also, I would add, *imperative*. The ethics of shared flow suggested here is a Spinozan take on aqueous embodiment. First, it involves sliding rather than facing, dwelling in clinamen as an ethical stance. Here there is no Levinasian face of the Other – there is no Other in the continuum, no Other on Robinson's island of Speranza.[22] Whatever faces are left, they are corroded by the millennia of water rushing over them – corroded to the smoothness of a rock. Second, this ethics involves openness without waiting, openness encountered in the certainty that justice is already embodied in the water we all are. This openness turns away from exchange and towards the water of the continuum: there is no waiting for the grace to be returned, but there is safety in the knowledge that it will be carried by waves to shores also inhabited by us. Third, an ethical continuum is involved where one's own body of water can never thrive unless others around also thrive. So, incline closer to bodies of water that benefit the continuum. Float away from bodies of water that are noxious to the continuum. Slide along bodies of water that allow new emergences. Dissolve yourself and become one with the without. Fourth, there is shared flow as freedom – but a freedom determined immanently, in accordance with the movement of the body among other bodies.

6

'The body exceeds the body or fails.'[23]

Michel Serres reminds us of the need to overflow or perish. Everything needs to pass, even our hydrobodies. As the Black feminist theorist Alexis Pauline Gumbs writes, '[y]es. I need a dorsal fin to navigate all of this transformation . . . In water that is always moving, having a dorsal fin provides balance, autonomy, and support for the swift turns you might have to make in this oceanic life.'[24] The hydrohuman is extending diagonally across and beyond Hydrogeos, but hesitantly, fitting in rather than dominating, sliding rather than swimming, perpetually wondering whether this is regression or progress.

Being hydrohuman is not about controlling but about accepting one's position in the surrounding watery collapse. The hydrohuman makes a home in this inclined planet and tends towards a horizontality that might drown the old humanity. The hydrohuman opens up, loves all the heads, becomes all the extensions. The hydrohuman is ushered into 'poly-river-amory',[25] polycules of overlapping lakes,[26] queer aqueous proximity,[27] more-than-human aqueous promiscuity.

A hydrohuman is a shallow water diver, an upside-down acrobat, rain, mist, plankton.

Becoming hydrohuman is our ultimate methodological instance of hydrojustice.

Wavewriting V

A Contract unto Hydrojustice

*This **Contract** is entered into by and among A, B, C, and C*, all bodies of water, hereafter referred to as 'the waters'.*

1. ***Purpose.*** *By means of this Contract, the waters embody textually their intention to slide next to one another in horizontality, to the extent that this sliding is desirable and sufficient to adumbrate their continuous flow (hereafter 'flow').*
2. ***Governing Affect.*** *The terms of this Contract shall be governed by and construed in accordance with the polyamorous ethics of shared flow. Erotic love does not have to bond all waters. However, the ethics of shared flow needs to bond all waters at all times.*

3. ***The Waters.*** *A, B, and C are interchangeable positions of becoming elemental and shall always operate as the basis of polyamorous resistance to verticality and synthetic infidelity. Non-synthetic Three is the core of the waters even when they are reduced to Two. C* on the other hand are always in the plural, are always placed in constellations of A, B, and C, and include all potential waters ('all waters are also potential contractual waters').*
4. ***Continuum and Ruptures.*** *All waters are collective. All waters shall respect the aquatic continuum both with one another and with the larger body of water. Yet each water may rupture away and slide separately, in liquid, solid, or vaporous form, thus becoming 'other'. This does not sever their continuum with the waters but only provides a temporary quickening into difference, and as such can be extended indefinitely.*
5. ***Horizontality.*** *All waters aim at the horizontality of doing and becoming. Verticality is discouraged. Unequal affective powers are to be treated with gentleness. Fragility is to be cherished.*
6. ***Writing.*** *All relationships among the waters shall be material and textual at the same time.*

All textuality is flesh. All flesh is sexual. All sexuality is aquatic. Texts shall populate the flow in trails of fleshy affect.

7. **Promiscuity.** *All waters are of all waters. No water belongs to any water. All waters can incline towards each other and exclude other waters, provided that horizontality and continuum are upheld and hydrojustice remains the defining ontological condition.*
8. **Property.** *The maintenance of the clinamen is the only property of concern here; it is proper to all waters and settled in an external impropriety. The clinamen forms part of a larger shared flow. It is constituted by the waters, and in turn constitutes the waters, expanding and shrinking along the pulsing flows of desire.*
9. **Validity, Amendment, and Revocation.** *Nothing in this Contract is binding, yet everything herein contributes to the bonding of the waters. Nothing can be resolved by evocation of this Contract. This Contract may be amended or modified by any water, yet the flow remains a collective responsibility. This Contract may be revoked at any point, even silently, on the basis of the maxim that love precedes law.*

WAVEWRITING

10. **Watermarks.** *The marks below represent the waters' acknowledgement that they are aware and willing to keep on repositioning themselves in hydrojust ways.*

Watermark of A   *Watermark of B*

Watermark of C   *Watermark of C*[*28]

Notes

Notes to Chapter 1

1 Ninety-seven per cent of the planet is occupied by water in its various forms: C. Ward, *Reflected in Water* (London: Cassell, 1997), 32.
2 'Water does rather than is. It wets, humidifies, evaporates, crystallizes, permeates, fills, leaks, drips, trickles, softens, hardens, congeals, dilutes, shapes, drills, erodes, corrodes, bonds, dissolves, buoys, transports, conducts, reflects, hides, reveals, refracts, diffracts, circulates, depletes, repletes, facilitates, blocks, disrupts, cools, heats, and more. In its protean capacity it forms into flows, tides, waves, currents, whirlpools, pools, drops, streams, oceans, and more.' E. Macura-Nnamdi and T. Sikora, 'Water', *Angelaki*, 28.1 (2023): 1–3, here 1.
3 A. Hickey, 'Waves Will Always Be Louder than Bombs', *OceanArchive.org*, 10 May 2024. https://ocean-archive.org/story/waves-will-always-be-louder-than-bombs.
4 M. Rodoreda, *Death in Spring*, trans. Martha Tennent (London: Penguin, 2018), 83.
5 E.g. the UN Human Rights Committee decision that the 'feelings of communion with deceased relatives' that were violated by climate change are to be respected:

18 September 2023, CCPR/C/135/D/3624/2019, at 8.2; see also the Indigenous-led campaign for the rights of nature, as a result of which many rivers, from Whanganui in 2017 to the Amazon in 2023, have been granted personhood.

6 M. Tomba, 'Social Property in the Cochabamba Water War, Bolivia 2000', *Angelaki*, 28.1 (2023): 73–86, here 79.

7 A. Philippopoulos-Mihalopoulos, *Spatial Justice: Body, Lawscape, Atmosphere* (London: Routledge, 2014).

8 V. I. Vernadsky, *History of Natural Waters* [in Russian] (Moscow: Nauka, 2003), as quoted in O. Chudaev et al., 'V. I. Vernadsky and Main Research Avenues in Modern Hydrogeochemistry', *Procedia Earth and Planetary Science*, 7 (2013): 163–167, here 163 (in Chudaev et al.'s translation).

9 A. Wafer and A. Pavoni, 'Liquidscapes of the City', *Lo Squaderno: Overflow*, 52 (2019): 61–65, here 64.

10 P. Linebaugh and M. Rediker, *The Many-Headed Hydra: The Hidden History of the Revolutionary Atlantic* (Boston, MA: Beacon, 2001).

11 M. Sheldrake, *Entangled Life* (New York: Random House, 2020), loc. 839.

12 '[T]o push their way through asphalt, a mushroom must inflate with water. For this to happen, water must travel rapidly through the network from one place to another and flow into a developing mushroom in a carefully directed pulse.' Ibid., loc. 958.

13 See e.g. P. Goodrich, 'Aquatopia: Lines of Amity and Laws of the Sea', in A. Carty and J. Nijman (eds), *Morality and Responsibility of Rulers* (Oxford: Oxford

University Press, 2018); R. Mawani, *Across Oceans of Law* (Durham, NC: Duke University Press, 2018).
14 Goodrich, 'Aquatopia', 212.
15 I. Calvino, *Le città invisibili* (Milan: Arnoldo Mondadori, 1993).
16 S. Alaimo, 'Violet–Black', in J. Cohen (ed.), *Prismatic Ecology* (Minneapolis: University of Minnesota Press, 2013), 234.
17 For K. Barad, *Meeting the Universe Halfway: Quantum Physics and the Entanglement of Matter and Meaning* (Durham, NC: Duke University Press, 2007), intra-action involves an entanglement with no a priori, except perhaps for entanglement itself.
18 F. Mazzara, 'Spaces of Visibility for the Migrants of Lampedusa', *Italian Studies*, 70.4 (2015): 449–464, here 452.
19 M. Jue, *Wild Blue Media* (Durham, NC: Duke University Press, 2020), 7.
20 M. Davies, *Law Unlimited: Materialism, Pluralism, and Legal Theory* (London: Routledge, 2017), 129.
21 B. Casavecchia, 'A Marine Thirst', in B. Casavecchia (ed.), *Thus Waves Come in Pairs: Thinking with the Mediterraneans* (London: Sternberg Press, 2023), xiii.
22 Perhaps the most relevant publication is C. Chen, J. MacLeod, and A. Neimanis (eds), *Thinking with Water* (Montreal: McGill-Queen's University Press, 2013).
23 'The substance of the human is ultimately inseparable from "the environment".' S. Alaimo, *Bodily Natures: Science, Environment, and the Material Self* (Bloomington: Indiana University Press, 2010), 2.

24 'Water not only flows between, and connects bodies; it also facilitates new kinds of bodies.' A. Neimanis, *Bodies of Water: Posthuman Feminist Phenomenology* (London: Bloomsbury, 2017), 96.
25 Mawani, *Across Oceans of Law*.
26 K. Amimoto Ingersoll, *Waves of Knowing: A Seascape Epistemology* (Durham, NC: Duke University Press, 2016).
27 P. Steinberg and K. Peters, 'The Ocean in Excess: Towards a More-than-Wet Ontology', *Dialogues in Human Geography*, 9.3 (2019): 293–307.
28 B. Spinoza, *Ethics*, trans. G. Parkinson (Oxford: Oxford University Press, 2000).
29 Ibid.
30 J. Kwong, 'Be Water: Insights into the Hong Kong Citizen Protest Movement', *Zeitgeister*, December 2020. https://www.goethe.de/prj/zei/en/art/22072105.html.

Notes to Chapter 2

1 But you can get shot *by* water: J. Anderlini, 'Hong Kong's "Water Revolution" Spins out of Control', *Financial Times*, 2 September 2019.
2 P. Yu, 'Be Water, My Friend: Protest, Identity Politics, and Democracy in Hong Kong', in S. A. Rahman et al. (eds), *Globalizing Political Theory* (London: Routledge, 2022).
3 G. Deleuze and F. Guattari, *A Thousand Plateaus: Capitalism and Schizophrenia*, trans. B. Massumi (London: Athlone Press, 1988), 353.

4 A. Katwala, 'How Long Droughts Make Flooding Worse', *WIRED*, 19 August 2022. https://www.wired.com/story/drought-causing-floods.
5 J. Roitman, *Anti-Crisis* (Durham, NC: Duke University Press, 2013).
6 E. DeLoughrey, 'Ordinary Futures', in E. DeLoughrey, Jill Didur, and Anthony Carrigan (eds), *Global Ecologies and the Environmental Humanities* (London: Routledge, 2015), 353.
7 D. Chandler, *Ontopolitics in the Anthropocene* (London: Routledge, 2018), 18.
8 J. Goodell, *The Water Will Come: Rising Seas, Sinking Cities, and the Remaking of the Civilized World* (New York: Little, Brown and Company, 2017), cover.
9 S. Freud, *Civilization and Its Discontents*, trans. J. Riviere (London: Hogarth Press, 1930), 66.
10 A. Neimanis, 'Alongside the Right to Water, a Posthumanist Feminist Imaginary', *Journal of Human Rights and the Environment*, 5.1 (2014): 5–24, here 15. See also V. Strang, 'Conceptual Relations: Water, Ideologies, and Theoretical Subversions', in Chen et al., *Thinking with Water*.
11 Neimanis, *Bodies of Water*, 96.
12 J. Pugliese, 'Bodies of Water', *Heat*, 12 (2006): 13–20, here 14.
13 Paraphrasing Merleau-Ponty (for whom the whole world is flesh): 'Where are we to put the limit between the body and the world, since the world is flesh?' M. Merleau-Ponty, *The Visible and the Invisible*, trans. A. Lingis (Evanston, IL: Northwestern University Press, 1968) 138.

14 E. Glissant, *Traité du Tout-Monde* (Paris: Gallimard, 1997), 194.
15 Glissant, *Traité*, 31.
16 H. Orrell and N. Zuo, 'When Sea Levels Rise, So Does Your Rent'. BBC News, 28 November 2023. https://www.bbc.com/news/world-67418276.
17 C. Jung, *Archetypes and the Collective Unconscious*, trans. G. Adler and R. Hull (Princeton, NJ: Princeton University Press, 1959).
18 T. Brennan, *The Transmission of Affect* (Ithaca, NY: Cornell University Press, 2004).
19 Visit www.ombudsman.europa.eu/en/doc/correspondence/en/182671.
20 D. Carrington, 'We Asked 380 Top Climate Scientists', *The Guardian*, 8 May 2024. www.theguardian.com/environment/ng-interactive/2024/may/08/hopeless-and-broken-why-the-worlds-top-climate-scientists-are-in-despair.
21 E. Glissant, *Poetics of Relation*, trans. B. Wing (Ann Arbor: University of Michigan Press, 2010). 6.
22 C. Sharpe, *In the Wake: On Blackness and Being* (Durham, NC: Duke University Press, 2016).
23 *Gregson v Gilbert* (1783) 99 ER 629. See also the whole issue 39 of *The Funambulist*, January 2022 ('A Political History of the Ocean').
24 M. N. Philip, *Zong!* (Hartford, CT: Wesleyan University Press, 2008).
25 *Gregson v Gilbert* 631; see T. T. Arvind, '"Though It Shocks One Very Much": Formalism and Pragmatism in the Zong and Bancoult', *Oxford Journal of Legal Studies*, 32.1 (2012): 113–151.

26 Glissant, *Traité*, 29.
27 I am grateful to Ewa Macura-Nnamdi for this formulation.
28 O. Tinsley, 'Black Atlantic, Queer Atlantic: Queer Imaginings of the Middle Passage', *GLQ: A Journal of Lesbian and Gay Studies*, 14.2/3 (2008): 191–215, here 197.
29 O. Equiano, 'The Interesting Narrative of the Life of Olaudah Equiano', in H. Gates Jr (ed.), *The Classic Slave Narratives* (New York: Penguin, 1987), 32.
30 Tinsley, 'Black Atlantic', 199.
31 B. Nascimento, *The Dialectic Is in the Sea* (Princeton, NJ: Princeton University Press, 2023), 323.
32 Visit https://andreaspm.com/show/touched-by-the-ghost-the-royal-cast-collection-copenhagen.
33 https://www.virgin-islands-history.org/en/timeline/danish-decision-to-abolish-transatlantic-slavetrade. See also N. A. T. Hall, *Slave Society in the Danish West Indies* (Mona: The University of the West Indies Press, 1992).
34 Visit https://stthomassource.com/content/2013/12/11/denmark-nixes-slavery-apology-reparations.
35 J. Nymann, *The Past Here to Stay*, 10, loop, single channel, 2019. This is a sound installation made specifically for the event.
36 S. E. Green-Pedersen and P. C. Willemoes Jørgensen, 'Dansk Kolonihistorie: Det Globale Perspektiv', in P. H. Jensen et al. (eds), *Dansk Kolonihistorie* (Århus: Forlaget Historia, 1983).
37 Visit https://en.natmus.dk/historical-knowledge/historical-themes/danish-colonies/the-danish-west-indies slavery.

38 Extract from Andreas Philippopoulos-Mihalopoulos' recent novel *Our Distance Became Water* (London: Eris / Columbia University Press, 2024), pp. 241–2.

Notes to Chapter 3

1 G. Bataille, *Theory of Religion* (New York: Zone Books, 1989), 19.
2 Neimanis, *Bodies of Water*, 1.
3 P. Glasgow, *The Concept of Water* (London: R. Glasgow Books, 2009), 174.
4 S. Alaimo, 'Jellyfish Science, Jellyfish Aesthetics: Posthuman Reconfigurations of the Sensible', in Chen, *Thinking with Water*, 153.
5 J.-M. Gili and F. Pages, 'Les Proliferacions de Meduses/ Jellyfish Blooms', *El Bolletí de la Societat d'Història Natural de les Balears,* 48 (2005), here 16.
6 D. Rothe, 'Jellyfish Encounters', *Critical Studies on Security*, 8.2 (2020): 145–159, here 151.
7 Alaimo, 'Jellyfish Science', 154.
8 G. Deleuze, *Essays Critical and Clinical*, trans. D. Smith (Minneapolis: University of Minnesota Press, 1997), 127–128.
9 E. R. Johnson, 'Governing Jellyfish: Eco-Security and "Life" in the Anthropocene', in I. Braverman (ed.), *Animals, Biopolitics, Law: Lively Legalities* (London: Routledge, 2016), 62.
10 Alaimo, 'Jellyfish Science', 154.
11 E. Tamalet Talbayev, 'Hydropower: Residual Dwelling between Life and Nonlife', *Angelaki* 28.1 (2023): 9–21, here 14.

12 S. Shapin, 'Story of Eau', *London Review of Books*, 46.13, 4 July 2024.
13 A. Neimanis, *Bodies of Water*, 29.
14 N. Boucquey et al., 'The Ontological Politics of Marine Spatial Planning', *Geoforum*, 75 (2016): 1–11, here 8.
15 C. Bannon, 'A Short Introduction to Roman Water Law', *Memoirs of the American Academy in Rome* 66 (2021): 1–18, here 1.
16 Neimanis, *Bodies of Water*, 16.
17 G. Anidjar, 'Learning Waters', *Angelaki*, 28.1 (2023): 99–110, here 106.
18 B. Casavecchia, 'A Marine Thirst', in Casavecchia, *Thus Waves Come in Pairs*, xv.
19 M. Stelder, 'A Sinking Empire', *Angelaki*, 28.1 (2023): 53–72, here 54.
20 Orrell and Zuo, 'When Sea Levels Rise, So Does Your Rent'.
21 Ibid.
22 O. Durmusoğlu, 'Hope the Voyage Is a Long One', in Casavecchia, *Thus Waves Come in Pairs*, 89.
23 T. Morrison, 'The Site of Memory', in W. Zinsser (ed.), *Inventing the Truth: The Art and Craft of Memoir* (Boston, MA: Houghton Mifflin, 1994), 83–102.
24 G. Deleuze, *Difference and Repetition*, trans. P. Patton (London: Continuum, 2004), 2.
25 Tamalet Talbayev, 'Hydropower', 10.
26 A. Hameed, 'Sea Changes and Other Futurisms', in H. Gunkel and A. Hameed (eds), *Visual Cultures as Time Travel* (London: Sternberg Press, 2021), 49.
27 M. J. Alexander, *Pedagogies of Crossing: Meditations*

on Feminism, Sexual Politics, Memory, and the Sacred (Durham, NC: Duke University Press, 2005).

28 Neimanis, *Bodies of Water*, 52.

29 J. MacLeod, 'Water and the Material Imagination: Reading the Sea of Memory against the Flows of Capital', in Chen, *Thinking with Water*, 49.

30 Recently developed tech systems that quantify historical emissions of companies led Vermont to be the first US state to introduce a law that holds fossil fuel companies accountable for their role in climate change and demands that they share the costs of climate change mitigation: A. Williams and J. Smyth, 'US State Passes Law to Make Oil Groups Pay for Climate Harm', *Financial Times*, 1 June 2024, 2.

31 N. Wilson and J. Inkster, 'Respecting Water: Indigenous Water Governance', *Environment and Planning E*, 1.4 (2018): 516–538, here 525.

32 F. Nietzsche, *Thus Spoke Zarathustra*, trans. G. Parkes (Oxford: Oxford University Press, 2005), 175.

33 Visit https://www.theguardian.com/science/2024/mar/08/astronomers-detect-waterworld-with-a-boiling-ocean-in-deep-space.

34 Visit https://www.nasa.gov/specials/ocean-worlds.

35 Visit https://www.sciencetimes.com/articles/47586/20231211/12-billion-year-old-largest-water-reservoir-universe-discovered-floating.htm.

36 Visit https://www.nasa.gov/specials/ocean-worlds.

37 From his third homily: τὸ ὕδωρ ὕδωρ νοήσωμεν. Basilius Magnus, *Hexaemeron*, Homiliae, 3.9.

38 Long Man is the personification of running water in Cherokee.

39 J. F. Kilpatrick and A. G. Kilpatrick, *The Shadow of Sequoyah: Social Documents of the Cherokees, 1862–1964* (Norman: University of Oklahoma Press, 1965), 80–81.
40 J. F. Kilpatrick and A. G. Kilpatrick, *Notebook of a Cherokee Shaman* (Washington, DC: Smithsonian Institution, 1970), 105.

Notes to Chapter 4

1 Visit https://eu.usatoday.com/story/news/factcheck/2022/05/10/fact-check-atlantic-pacific-oceans-mix-regardless-clay-and-iron/9652991002.
2 A. Omstedt, *A Philosophical View of the Ocean and Humanity* (Cham: Springer, 2020).
3 Deleuze, *Difference and Repetition*, 200: 'It is the original determination of the direction of movement, the synthesis of movement and its direction which relates one atom to another.'
4 Neimanis, *Bodies of Water*, 96.
5 Barad, *Meeting the Universe Halfway*.
6 N. Sharpe, *Saltwater People* (Crows Nest: Allen &Unwin, 2002), 38.
7 A. Bispo dos Santos, *A terra dá, a terra quer* (São Paulo: Ubu Editora, 2023), 8–9, as translated and quoted by my colleague and former doctoral student Renan Nery Porto, *A Viscous Law and the Sticky Bodies of Cocoa: For a Cosmopoetics of Justice*, University of Westminster Research Depository, 2024.
8 D. Zanchettin et al., 'Sea-level Rise in Venice: Historic and Future Trends', *Natural Hazards and Earth System*

Sciences, 21 (2021): 2643–2678. https://doi.org/10.5194/nhess-21-2643-2021.

9 The first fifteen floodgate closures, until January 2021, contributed to a reduction in marsh deposition and increase in channel infilling, with serious consequences for geomorphic diversity: D. Tognin et al., 'Loss of Geomorphic Diversity in Shallow Tidal Embayments', *Science Advances*, 8.13 (2022): 1–12.

10 D. Tognin et al., 'Marsh Resilience to Sea-Level Rise Reduced by Storm-Surge Barriers in the Venice Lagoon', *Nature Geoscience*, 14 (2021): 906–911.

11 D. Tagliapietra and G. Umgiesser, 'Venice and Its Lagoon *fin de siècle*', *Regional Environmental Change* 23(4) (2023), 125.

12 E. Glasberg, *Antarctica as Cultural Critique: The Gendered Politics of Scientific Exploration and Climate Change* (New York: Palgrave Macmillan, 2012), xiii.

13 Visit https://www.theguardian.com/world/2020/jun/20/cultural-tabu-how-an-ancient-ocean-custom-is-saving-fijis-reefs.

14 M. Ntona and M. Schröder, 'Regulating Oceanic Imaginaries', *Maritime Studies*, 19 (2020): 241–254.

15 Goodrich, 'Aquatopia', 207. This is also the reason why, in *Nomos*, Carl Schmitt famously ignored the sea, albeit from a different political perspective: 'The sea has no character, in the original sense of the word, which comes from the Greek *charassein*, meaning to engrave, to scratch, to imprint. . . . On the waves there is nothing but waves.' Carl Schmitt, *The Nomos of the Earth in the International Law of the Jus Publicum Europaeum* (New York: Telos, 2003), 42–3.

16 Goodrich, 'Aquatopia', 217.
17 Ibid.
18 P. Steinberg and K. Peters, 'Wet Ontologies, Fluid Spaces: Giving Depth to Volume through Oceanic Thinking', *Environment and Planning D: Society and Space*, 33 (2015): 247–264, here 259.
19 J. Cheever, 'The Swimmer', *New Yorker*, 10 July 1964. https://www.newyorker.com/magazine/1964/07/18/the-swimmer.
20 T. Woods, 'A Life in the Day: The Masculine Irreality of *The Swimmer*', *Bright Wall/Dark Room*, 64, October 2018. https://www.brightwalldarkroom.com/2018/10/12/the-swimmer-1968.
21 Amimoto Ingersoll, *Waves of Knowing*.
22 J. Chow and M. Urcaregui, 'Just Keep Swimming?' *Angelaki* 28.1 (2023): 36–52, here 43.
23 G. Deleuze, 'Sur Spinoza: Cours Vincennes, 17 mars 1981', in L. Lambert, *Spinoza* (New York: The Funambulist/Punctum, 2013).
24 L. Strauss, 'Interpretation of Genesis', *L'Homme*, 21(1) (1981), 5–20, 11.
25 Visit https://www.tuvalu.tv.
26 I. Duncan, 'Necro-Hydrology', *e-flux Architecture*, June 2023. https://www.e-flux.com/architecture/hydroreflexivity/543089/necro-hydrology. See also I. Duncan and S. Levidis, 'Weaponizing a River', *e-flux Architecture*, April 2020.
27 Visit https://thefishsite.com/articles/a-visit-to-the-octopus-farming-pioneers-nueva-pescanova.
28 'In fact there is no scientifically validated knowledge about the "intelligence" of the octopus, or whether it

is more or less intelligent than other species already bred.' Bill Chappell, NPR, 7 February 2024. https://www.npr.org/2024/02/07/1229233837/octopus-farm-spain-controversy.

29 A. Hickey, 'Waves Will Always Be Louder than Bombs', *Ocean Archive*, 2024, https://ocean-archive.org/story/waves-will-always-be-louder-than-bombs.

30 K. Eshun, *More Brilliant than the Sun: Adventures in Sonic Fiction* (London: Quartet Books, 1998), 83.

31 Visit https://www.economist.com/science-and-technology/2018/04/21/a-group-of-people-with-an-amphibious-life-have-evolved-traits-to-match.

32 Amimoto Ingersoll, *Waves of Knowing*, 72.

33 Neimanis, *Bodies of Water*, 148–149.

34 A reimagined version of the opening story in Andreas Philippopoulos-Mihalopoulos, *Book of Water* (London: Eris/Columbia University Press, 2023).

35 W. Adams et al., 'Water, Rules and Gender: Water Rights in an Indigenous Irrigation System, Marakwet, Kenya', *Development and Change*, 28 (1997): 707–730, here 719.

36 A. Craft and L. King, 'Building the Treaty #3 Nibi Declaration Using an Anishinaabe Methodology of Ceremony, Language and Engagement', *Water*, 13 (2021): 532–547, here 532.

37 Goodrich, 'Aquatopia', 219.

38 Extract from Jan Hogan, 'A Touching "Contract"', in C. Nirta et al. (eds), *Law and the Senses: Touch* (London: University of Westminster Press, 2020), 89–91.

Notes to Chapter 5

1 I. Calvino, *Mr. Palomar*, trans. W. Weaver (London: Martin Secker & Warburg, 1985), 12.
2 On wave diffraction, see Barad, *Meeting the Universe Halfway*, 74.
3 His is what Stefan Helmreich calls 'the *chronic* ocean': 'The repetition and churn of such a sea is unevenly distributed, socially intensified, and felt. It is choppy, subject, like waves, to cluttered, broken motion.' S. Helmreich, *A Book of Waves* (Durham, NC: Duke University Press, 2023), 19.
4 R. Gardner, *The Art of Body Surfing* (Chester: Chilton, 1972), 42.
5 R. Wong, 'Untapping Watershed Mind', in Chen, *Thinking with Water*, 266.
6 M. Serres, *Genesis*, trans. G. James and J. Nielson (Ann Arbor: University of Michigan Press, 1995).
7 W. Ming-Yi, *The Man with the Compound Eyes*, trans. D. Sterk (London: Vintage, 2014), 169.
8 *Vanuatu Women's Water Music*, dir. T. Cole. Port Vila: Further Arts, 2014. Documentary.
9 I am indebted to Cristina Hernández and her work on the Magdalena river in Colombia for this insight.
10 Amimoto Ingersoll, *Waves of Knowing*, 45.
11 Wong, 'Untapping Watershed Mind', 264.
12 J. Pugliese, 'Intercorporeity of Animated Water', *Angelaki*, 28.1 (2023): 22–35, here 24.
13 A. Philippopoulos-Mihalopoulos, 'Flesh of the Law: Material Metaphors', *Journal of Law and Society* , 43.1 (2016): 45–65. See also D. Gandorfer and Z. Ayub,

'Matterphorical', *Theory & Event*, 24.1 (2021): 2–13, on the whole issue of 'matterphor'.

14 G. Deleuze, *The Logic of Sense*, trans. M. Lester (London: Continuum, 2004), 11.

15 J. MacLeod, 'Water and the Material Imagination: Reading the Sea of Memory against the Flows of Capital', in Chen, *Thinking with Water*, 49.

16 A. Riehl, 'The Rising Ocean Will Extinguish More Than Land: It Will Kill Entire Languages', *The Guardian*, 28 June 2023, https://www.theguardian.com/environment/2023/jun/28/indigenous-languages-climate-crisis-threat-pacific-islands.

17 Amimoto Ingersoll, *Waves of Knowing*, 93.

18 G. Bachelard, *Water and Dreams*, trans. E. Farrell (Dallas, TX: Pegasus Foundation, 1983) 15.

19 Wilson and Inkster, 'Respecting Water', 523.

20 I. Nehme, 'To Live to Tell Another Tale', in Casavecchia, *Thus Waves Come in Pairs*, 105.

21 M. Chandler and A. Neimanis, 'Water and Gestationality: What Flows beneath Ethics', in Chen, *Thinking with Water*, 62.

22 G. Deleuze, 'Une théorie d'autrui (autrui, Robinson et le pervers)', *Critique* 241 (1967): 503–525.

23 M. Serres, *The Five Senses: A Philosophy of Mingled Bodies*, trans. M. Sankey and P. Cowley (London: Continuum, 2008), 307.

24 A. P. Gumbs, *Undrowned: Black Feminist Lessons from Marine Mammals* (Chico, CA: AK Press, 2020), 22.

25 K. TallBear, 'Poly-River-Amory: An Excerpt from the Non-Monogamy Letters'. Unsettle, 10 December

2023. https://kimtallbear.substack.com/p/poly-river-amory-an-excerpt-from.
26 L. Boyle, 'Think of a Polycule as a Complex Lake System'. Ready for Polyamory (blog), 3 February 2021. https://www.readyforpolyamory.com/post/think-of-a-polycule-as-a-complex-lake-system.
27 J. Chow and B. Bushman, 'Hydro-Eroticism', *English Language Notes*, 57.1 (2019): 96–115.
28 This is a reimagined version of A. Philippopoulos-Mihalopoulos, 'A Contract unto Love, or Entering into Polyamorous Love with Goodrich', *Law, Culture and the Humanities*, May 2024. https://doi.org/10.1177/17438721241249685. The original piece is based on the legal philosopher Peter Goodrich's work on law and love. While writing this book, I realised that love, just like justice, is nothing if not hydrolove, and I am horizontally grateful to Peter for this realisation.